The Rise and Fall of Democracy in
Early America, 1630-1789

The Rise and Fall of Democracy

in Early America, 1630-1789

The Legacy for Contemporary Politics

Joshua Miller

The Pennsylvania State University Press
University Park, Pennsylvania

Library of Congress Cataloging–in–Publication Data

Miller, Joshua I.
    The rise and fall of democracy in early America, 1630–1789 : the
legacy for contemporary politics / Joshua I. Miller.
        p.   cm.
    Includes bibliographical references and index.
    ISBN 0-271-00744-3
        1. United States—Politics and government—Colonial period, ca.
1600–1775.   2. United States—Politics and government—1775–1783.
3. United States—Politics and government—1783–1789.   4. Political
culture—United States—History.   5. Democracy—History.   I. Title.
JK54.M55   1991
321.8'042'0973—dc20   90-46819
                                                                                    CIP

It is the policy of The Pennsylvania State University Press to use
acid-free paper for the first printing of all clothbound books.
Publications on uncoated stock satisfy the minimum requirements of
American National Standard for Information Sciences—Permanence of
Paper for Printed Library Materials, ANSI Z39.48–1984.

To
John Schaar, Sheldon Wolin, and Wilson Carey McWilliams

Contents

Acknowledgments

This book would still be in a drawer if my friend Charles Hersch had not called me from California and asked to see it to help him prepare his lectures for a course on American Political Thought. After a perusal, he suggested that some larger portion of the public might want to read it. That had never occurred to me, and I am grateful to Chuck for the suggestion. Much of what is good in this book is due to his editorial work on it.

I want to thank my parents, not only for life itself and for love and support ever since, but also for serving as examples of the public life advocated by democratic theorists. They have lived lives of compassion, integrity, and extraordinary commitment to political ideals. My mother, Joyce, is a national leader of the trade union movement, and my father, Jay, is a career official with the American Civil Liberties Union. Although they will disagree with many of the political positions expressed herein, I think that we are ultimately on the same side, and I hope that I can still come over for dinner.

By the end of John Schaar's second lecture on American Political Thought at the University of California, Santa Cruz, in 1973, I knew that I had found a new political philosophy. Only later did I realize that I had also found a mentor and a vocation. Professor Schaar's eloquence, knowledge, wit, and humanity have inspired me since I met him. Schaar not only suggested the topic for this book but, especially in its early form, made many useful suggestions for revisions and additions.

After college, I wrote to Schaar from Jonesboro, Arkansas, where I was a community organizer, to ask his advice about graduate school. He recommended that I stick with public life for awhile rather than joining the academy, but if I insisted on going, then I should study with his friend Sheldon Wolin at Princeton. It was good advice.

Sheldon Wolin, now emeritus, was a great teacher of political theory, especially for graduate students. Every Wolin lecture was an intellectual event. Professor Wolin generously worked with me on my writing and thinking and articulated what was required of a graduate student and a scholar. Wolin's standards are so high that I take a certain comfort in knowing that I can never meet them, although they continue to serve as standards.

Maurice Natanson, professor of philosophy at Yale, has been a cherished teacher since I took his courses on existentialism and phenomenology at UCSC. Natanson has served as a patient guide at each crossroad of the journey. He has been for me, and for many students, a model of a humane teacher committed to the life of the mind.

Wilson Carey McWilliams has also been a teacher and friend since I attended his great lectures on American Political Thought at Rutgers while I was a graduate student at Princeton. I am grateful to him for finding something of value in my work and being willing to tell others about it. He and Michael Lienesch were the scholarly reviewers of my manuscript for

Penn State Press, and this book is much stronger for their criticisms and suggestions.

I thank Sanford G. Thatcher, director of Penn State Press, for his encouragement and graciousness. Jeffery Tulis, Aaron Bernstein, Seth Borgos, Wendy Brown, William Connolly, Jane Cullen, Sanford Kessler, Ernst Manasse, Nancy Schwartz, Peter Steinberger, Brian Weiner, and Eric Ziolkowski made helpful suggestions for revising the manuscript. Less direct but no less important aid and inspiration was provided by Ingrid Creppell, Marge Frantz, David Sachs, and Nicholas Xenos. I have appreciated the support of my colleagues and students at Lafayette College. Heather Kashner, a Charles A. Dana Research Assistant, provided crucial research aid and assisted in the preparation of the final manuscript.

Chapters 2 and 5 originally appeared, in somewhat different form, in, respectively, *The Journal of Politics* (University of Texas Press) and *Political Theory* (Sage Publications). I am grateful to the publishers of those journals for permission to reprint the essays here.

As noted above, I had lots of help, but writing this book was largely solitary work, and I have tried to write it in a spirit of intellectual independence.

The rhetoric of acknowledgments requires a paean here to spouse and child. Lacking both, I want to offer thanks to my family and friends, to whom I owe nearly all happiness in life.

*The Rise and Fall of Democracy in
Early America, 1630-1789*

1

Introduction

mericans are deeply divided, among themselves and within themselves, on the subject of democracy. Democracy is sometimes taken to be America's highest value, even its essence; but at other times, democracy is seen as America's nightmare. Democracy is the New England town meeting; democracy is the sheriff of a small southern town. Much of what is worst in America has been imputed to direct democracy. Pure democracy, it is said, means the persecution of the minority by the majority. Democracy leads to, among other things, prayer in schools; the banning, labeling, or burning of books and records; and restrictions on alcohol, drugs, sex, and abortion. Above all, democracy has produced racial segregation and discrimination. Some people implicate democracy when the city council

of Yonkers, New York, refuses to permit low-cost housing for blacks to be built in white neighborhoods.

On the other hand, most Americans retain an affection for the democratic ideal, even for its more radical elements. The image of people directly taking control of their lives in a town meeting still has positive connotations for many. We hate dictators, the domination of one country, or even one social group, by another, and censorship of speech and press. It is hardly controversial to say that adults should govern themselves and that government cannot be entrusted to experts.

The division over direct democracy has more than theoretical significance. Democratic themes are at the center of debates concerning abortion, affirmative action, welfare, and worker ownership and participation in decision making. In Tiananmen Square, Chinese students called for democracy, as did Solidarity in Poland and the reform movements in the Soviet Union.[1] In the United States, a number of political thinkers and activists have recently advocated direct democracy as the best standard for political change.[2] Centralized, hierarchical forms of government and economy in the United States, it is said, have undermined liberty; the power held now by the central government and the giant corporations should flow back to revived political communities. These new populists, direct democrats, or communitarians want to recover a form of politics where neighbors share power. They want ordinary people to be able to take control of their collective lives.

I do not intend to argue the case for democracy in this book. I have the more modest ambition of contributing to the greater understanding of the theoretical and historical dimen-

1. Lawrence Weschler, *Solidarity: Poland in the Season of Its Passion* (New York: Simon and Schuster, 1982); Adam Michnick, *Letters From Prison and Other Essays*, trans. M. Latynski (Berkeley: University of California Press, 1985).

2. In addition to the works referred to in the notes below, see Harry C. Boyte, *Backyard Revolution* (Philadelphia: Temple University Press, 1980); *The New Populism: The Politics of Enpowerment*, ed. Harry C. Boyte and Frank Riessman (Philadelphia: Temple University Press, 1986); Lawrence Goodwyn, *Democratic Promise: The Populist Moment in America* (New York: Oxford University Press, 1976); and Robert A. Dahl, *After the Revolution?* (New Haven: Yale University Press, 1970).

sions of today's discussions about democracy. I want to explore democracy's nature along with its problems and possibilities by examining that period of American history when mainstream political culture was highly democratic, the period before the ratification of the Constitution. I want to address questions like the following: What is democracy? What does a democratic political culture look like? What is the relationship of democracy to liberalism and conservatism? Perhaps the central theoretical questions of the book are these: What relationship does democracy posit between people and power? What are the implications of that relationship for thinking about new types of political practice and institutions?

I discuss these questions by examining the debate about democracy in early American politics. Yet, despite its historical approach, this is a book about political theory, not history. My aim is not primarily to reconstruct the origin and development of early American political practices through the use of primary materials, but rather to study certain discussions, texts, and moments of early America in order to shed light, however indirectly, upon the contemporary problem of democracy. The social and historical context of eighteenth-century thought interests me only insofar as the context illuminates the ideas.

I

While certain turns of my argument may be more appreciated by political theorists, I have tried to write a book that is comprehensible both to students and to activists who may have no special training in political theory. Some readers may find the book useful as a general introduction to American political thought and particularly to the subject of democracy.

Citizens and activists who pick up this book may wonder what a theoretical and historical essay has to offer them. Given the enormous amount of work to be done, and the short amount of time in which to do it, why bother with an academic book? I take the question seriously, and offer three answers: (1) to get a clearer picture of the ends for which democrats are working; (2) to better understand the obstacles posed to democracy by mainstream American politics and political thought; and (3) to attain the inspiration that can be provided to democrats by early American history and ideas.

I know from experience that in the daily life of the organizer or activist the big picture is frequently and necessarily obscured by quotidian tasks; nevertheless, an understanding of the nature of the political world and a vision of the type of society that one is striving to create are essential components of the political actor's knowledge. This essay attempts both to illuminate the character of American politics and to discuss the problems and possibilities of the democratic ideal. Neither, it seems to me, can be fully understood without attending to the debates over direct democracy held in the early period of American political thought.

Given my interest in addressing those who have a practical interest in democracy, it may seem odd that this book is historical and theoretical, rather than analytic and programmatic. Perhaps some organizer or pragmatically inclined student might say that what we need is not theory or history, but concrete proposals for change and guidelines for action. If the United States were to decentralize power, how would the military, the highway system, the national bureaucracy, and the corporation be reorganized? Should those who want to decentralize power work at the national or local level? These are important questions, but they are not the primary concern in this book. Those who are interested in examples of concrete proposals for democratic reform can find them in essays by John Schaar, Kirkpatrick Sale, Benjamin Barber, and others.[3]

3. John H. Schaar, *Legitimacy in the Modern State* (New Brunswick, N.J.: Transaction Press, 1981), 349–57; Kirkpatrick Sale, *Human Scale* (New York: Coward, McCann, and Geoghegan, 1980); Mark Satin, *New Age Politics* (New York: Delta, 1979); and Benjamin R. Barber, *Strong Democracy* (Berkeley: University of California Press, 1984), 261–311.

Instead of specific suggestions for change, I intend to acquaint democrats with their ancestors: localists should know that they have allies in the American tradition. They should take solace from learning that they are not alone, that other Americans, now concealed by time and neglect or deliberate misrepresentation, believed in and fought for the principle and practice of direct democracy. They should know that before the ratification of the Constitution there existed a remarkably rich democratic culture in America. When this legacy is discovered, the real stakes of early American politics become clearer, as does their relevance to contemporary concerns.

The struggle over the ratification of the Constitution was not merely a fight over abstract principles, but over a way of life that the Antifederalists identified with liberty and the Federalists considered weak, petty, and destructive of the two great aims of government: the forging of a mighty empire and the protection of individual rights, particularly property rights. Contemporary prejudices and arguments against direct democracy are, to a large extent, inheritances from the eighteenth-century battles. These battles were between decentralists like the Shays' Rebels, the Berkshire Constitutionalists, and the Antifederalists, all of whom sought to preserve the principles of participation, local autonomy, and political community, and those like the Federalists, who wanted to consolidate and centralize power in the new nation.

The sheer amount of democratic activity and thought in early America should inspire decentralists today. Proportionally, far more ordinary citizens participated in politics then than do now. The political communities that today would have to be revived or newly created were once a fundamental feature of American life; the idea of local self-rule was then an essential characteristic of American politics.

Contemporary democrats may be surprised to find that they have localist ancestors among the most forbidding of early Americans, the Puritans of Massachusetts Bay. However shameful their mistreatment of witches and Quakers, the Puritans

were localists who opposed the centralized, hierarchical organization of the Catholic and Anglican churches. The Puritans
developed an alternative theory of church organization that gave
power to the members of small, largely autonomous, congregations. The Puritans struggled with England to preserve the
charters that guaranteed their self-governance. Even within the
Puritan community, members struggled to make more mani-
fest those egalitarian and participatory impulses contained in
Puritan theology and church organization, political thought
and practice.

      Congregationalism was but the beginning of early
American democracy. Although not self-consciously democratic, the Puritans planted the seeds for more egalitarian communitarian movements of the eighteenth century. The American Revolution was a great impetus to popular action: colonial
leaders taught citizens that distant rule was illegitimate. Colonists were called upon to throw off their deferential attitudes
and establish through revolutionary action the fact that they
were free and equal men and women. This new democratic
consciousness was not easily forgotten, and after the Revolution the citizens demanded that the newly independent towns
and states embody the principles for which they had recently
battled. So at the Revolution's end, highly democratic state
constitutions were ratified by popularly elected conventions.
When colonial elites tried to reduce the power of the people and
to ignore their needs and will, the citizens engaged in frequent
and ferocious direct action. Each radically democratic movement faced powerful, articulate opponents, none of them more
formidable than the Federalists, the authors and advocates of
the United States Constitution.

II

I suspect that most people are unfamiliar with the nature of
early American direct democracy. Why is this so? First, direct

democracy is often presumed by authors of textbooks in American government and history to be undesirable, and thus little mention is made of it. Direct democracy, it is routinely asserted, is impractical in a large country and invariably threatens individual rights. Representative democracy is more pragmatic and more just. In this spirit, the Articles of Confederation are dismissed as unworkable, the Shays' Rebels are labeled a selfish or anarchistic faction. The textbooks assume that the Founding Fathers were great men of unquestionable wisdom, devoted to liberty above all else, so their opponents must surely have been wrong.

The citizenry has been misled by the textbooks, but even scholars are often unaware of the true nature of early American politics because they have been misdirected by some of the most eminent students of the field. Louis Hartz advanced the powerful, but too sweepingly applied, thesis in his great work, *The Liberal Tradition in America,* that nearly all of American politics and political thought has taken place in the room of Lockean liberalism.[4] Only those theorists and movements that advocated individual rights, particularly the right of private property, were admitted to the American political conversation. Genuine radicals and conservatives who put forward alternatives to liberalism have had, said Hartz, little place in the American political tradition. Hartz's thesis is largely correct. Most American political thought does begin with Lockean arguments. But Hartz went too far in denying the existence of genuinely radical elements of American political thought and practice.

Hartz is not alone. Most major scholars of American political thought have denied, rejected, or ignored radical democracy in the early period. Perry Miller in *Orthodoxy in Massachusetts* suggested that the American Puritans were not, at bottom, decentralists; they only developed a novel way to preserve Catholic and Anglican principles of uniformity. Han-

---

4. *The Liberal Tradition in America* (New York: Harcourt, Brace, and World, 1955); and "American Political Thought and the American Revolution," *American Political Science Review* 46 (June 1952): 321–42.

nah Arendt dismissed the radicals of the eighteenth century as a small group that did not appreciate the importance of creating stable institutions after the American Revolution. Herbert Storing contended that he looked in vain for novel ideas in the writings of the Antifederalists, but found in them only a variant of liberal individualism. Jackson Turner Main, a historian sympathetic to the Antifederalists, did describe them as "democrats," but he conflated democracy and liberalism so that the Antifederalists appeared to be militant liberals rather than radical democrats.[5] I will argue throughout the book that to understand the real nature of early American politics one must distinguish between democracy and liberalism.

III

The early period of American politics, particularly the Puritans and the democratic radicals of the eighteenth century, has been examined more often by historians and literary critics than by political theorists. Those examinations have generally blurred the line between democracy and liberalism, calling what was essentially liberalism "liberal democracy." My discussion employs a distinction between democracy and liberalism recently developed by political theorists.[6]

5. Orthodoxy in Massachusetts (Cambridge: Harvard University Press, 1933); Hannah Arendt, On Revolution (New York: Penguin Books, 1986 [1963]); What the Anti-Federalists Were For, vol. 1 of The Complete Anti-Federalist, 7 vols., ed. Herbert J. Storing (Chicago: University of Chicago Press, 1981); Jackson Turner Main, The Antifederalists (Chapel Hill: University of North Carolina Press, 1961).

6. See Sheldon S. Wolin, Politics and Vision (Boston: Little, Brown, 1960), 293–94 and passim, "The New Conservatives," New York Review of Books 23:1 (6 February 1976): 6–11, and "The People's Two Bodies," democracy 1:1 (January 1981): 9–24; Schaar, Legitimacy, esp. 53–55 and 193–209; Wilson Carey McWilliams, "Politics," American Quarterly 35 (1983): 19–38, esp. 27, and "Reinhold Niebuhr: New Orthodoxy for Old Liberalism," American Political Science Review 56 (1962): 874–85; Michael Paul Rogin, Ronald Reagan: The Movie (Berkeley: University of California Press, 1987), 134–41 and passim; and Barber, Strong Democracy.

Although the terms are frequently taken to be synonymous, democracy and liberalism actually refer to profoundly
different political ideals. Sometimes our leaders call any country
allied with the United States a democracy. At other times the
term refers to a government whose officials are popularly
elected for fixed terms and that gives due regard to individual
rights. I would call such a regime not democratic but "liberal,"
reserving the term "democracy" for what is commonly called
"direct democracy."

Missing from liberalism is what the ancient Greeks took
to be democracy's essential feature—the shaping and sharing of
a common life by citizens of equal power in a small community.
Thus, key elements of democracy include community, participation, a rough equality of power, a small territory, collective
autonomy, and a concern for the common good that takes
priority over private interest. This definition of democracy has
its origin in the Greek *polis;* in the ideal conception of the polis
a relatively small group of people were united by tradition,
affection, and a concern for their common welfare.[7] It was an
autonomous political body whose direction was set by the
citizens in the public assembly. By today's standards, the criteria
for citizenship in the polis seem unfairly restrictive, but the
Greeks were highly inclusive for their own time. No advocate
of political community whose ideals are derived from the polis
would today exclude women from citizenship or countenance
slavery, but they would like to find some way to recover the
crucial component of the polis: citizens sharing power and a
common way of life.

The democratic ideal implies the conditions of its exis-

7. See H. D. F. Kitto, *The Greeks* (New York: Penguin Books, 1957); Fustel de
Coulanges, *The Ancient City,* trans. W. Small (Baltimore: Johns Hopkins University
Press, 1980); M. I. Finley, *Economy and Society in Ancient Greece,* ed. B. D. Shaw and
R. P. Saller (New York: Viking, 1982), chaps. 1, 3, 5, and 6; Jean-Pierre Vernant, *The
Origins of Greek Thought* (Ithaca: Cornell University Press, 1982 [1962]), esp. chap. 4;
Martin Diamond, "Ethics and Politics: The American Way," in *The Moral Foundations
of the American Republic,* 2d ed. (Charlottesville: University Press of Virginia, 1977), 39–
72.

tence. In order to create political community, there must exist an approximate parity of wealth, a limited number of citizens, and a small territory. And in order for all to participate in political debate, democracy protects freedom of speech. Democracy can exist only in a small state, says political theorist Wilson Carey McWilliams, because only there will citizens be able to directly participate in politics and be willing to make sacrifices for the public good.[8] "Participation," writes McWilliams, "requires small communities where citizens can hear and be heard, and a politics suited to the slow pace of deliberation." In the small state the belief in the common good, necessary to hold the community together when its members disagree on particular issues, will be tangible, within the range of the citizens' senses. Democracy, because of its inextricable ties with political community, requires "stable relations that can foster mutual knowledge and trust."[9] In many ways, democracy is a deeply conservative doctrine. In the chapters that follow, I will show that democracy has as many affinities with conservative political thought as with liberalism.

The democratic ideal can be clearly contrasted with the ideal of liberalism. Direct participation and equality of power are not essential elements of liberalism. Unlike democracy, liberalism is a revolutionary philosophy that encourages, through its protection of property rights and rejection of tradition, mobility and rapid technological change. Because community is not recognized as a necessary component of the good political order, a liberal government can exist, even flourish, in a very large territory. In liberalism the idea of a common good is transformed to that of a common interest—the belief that the self-interest of each, usually defined in material terms, will

8. *The Idea of Fraternity in America* (Berkeley: University of California Press, 1973), esp. 1–95; "Democracy and the Citizen: Community, Dignity, and the Crisis of Contemporary Politics in America," in *How Democratic Is the Constitution?*, ed. R. A. Goldwin and W. A. Schambra (Washington, D.C.: American Enterprise Institute, 1980), 79–101; and McWilliams, "Politics."
9. McWilliams, "Politics," 28.

promote the self-interest of all. Liberalism accepts, even encour-
·ages, the selfish demands of individuals and groups.[10]

Liberalism stands for, above all, individual rights and is
compatible with a strong state that is supposed to ensure those
rights. Since its initial formulation in the theoretical works of
Hobbes and Locke, liberalism has conceived of individuals as
fundamentally separate from the community. According to
political theorist Michael Rogin, liberalism implies "propertied
individualism" and "the independence of men, each from the
other and from cultural, traditional, and communal attach-
ments."[11] Liberalism is largely concerned with rights, privacy,
and property; democracy does not repudiate those things, but
has an equally high regard for political participation and the
common good. As formulated in the United States by disciples
of Jefferson and Paine, liberal thought has stressed the rights of
the individual against the state, but it has also defended individual rights even when those rights conflict with the common
good. Unlike liberals, advocates of direct democracy have no
instant solution when individual rights, majority rule, and the
common good come into conflict.

One of Sheldon Wolin's most important contributions
to the understanding of eighteenth-century American political
thought is the link that he has discovered between liberalism
and the state. Wolin has revealed that the founders of liberal
political thought were as preoccupied with the creation of a
powerful state as they were with protecting individual rights.[12]
Unlike liberalism, direct democracy is antithetical to the strong
state insulated from the lives of ordinary people.

In this book I want to look at some of the potentialities,
implications, and hidden aspects of direct democracy. Nevertheless, direct democracy is, I recognize, a controversial starting

10. See Wolin, *Politics and Vision*, esp. chaps. 1–4 and 10.
11. "Liberal Society and the Indian Question," in *Ronald Reagan: The Movie*,
135.
12. "The Idea of the State in America," *Humanities in Society* 3 (Spring 1980):
151–68, and *The Presence of the Past: Essays on the State and the Constitution* (Baltimore:
Johns Hopkins University Press, 1989).

point. Many political thinkers today dismiss the recovery of direct democracy as an unworkable ideal, and others believe that direct democracy is unnecessary. Let me briefly address those two objections.

IV

Critics of direct democracy often make three powerful points: (1) The experience of community can be attained without significantly altering American political arrangements. (2) Political power has become so nationalized and internationalized that localities can no longer hope for the autonomy of the Greek city-state. (3) Politics and economics have become so complex that ordinary human beings are now, whatever was the case before, incapable of directly controlling political power.

Many discussions of democracy begin by dismissing the polis as a perfectly charming ideal that has no relevance to politics in our own day. Robert Dahl, perhaps the most prominent contemporary political scientist concerned with democracy, has written:

> Today the polis vision may be seen by a few people as a beguiling form of political life; but as a reality and as an ideal it is in no sense fundamental to modern political culture, it is known mainly to specialists, and almost no one seriously proposes that the modern democratic nations be carved up into genuinely autonomous states.[13]

13. "The City in the Future of Democracy," *American Political Science Review* 61 (December 1967): 958. See also Robert A. Dahl and Ed Tufte, *Size and Democracy* (Stanford: Stanford University Press, 1973) and Dahl's *After the Revolution?, Democracy and Its Critics* (New Haven: Yale University Press, 1989), and *Dilemmas of Pluralist Democracy* (New Haven: Yale University Press, 1982).

Sociologist Robert Nisbet does not want to revive democracy or community, but he does hope to recover the
feelings of affection once associated with the word "community."[14] He yearns for the restoration of "moral values and
social relationships" that he says once existed under feudalism.
To achieve Nisbet's goals would not require a fundamental
restructuring of American politics; in fact, increasing the sense
of affinity among people, so sorely lacking in the large state,
would stabilize and strengthen the existing order. "Neither
science, nor technology, nor the city," Nisbet writes, "is
inherently incompatible with the existence of moral values and
social relationships which will do for modern man what the
extended family, the parish, and the village did for earlier
man."[15]

Nisbet's formulations are part of a tradition of American
political rhetoric that invokes values and ideas that once challenged mainstream politics and then incorporates those very
ideas into a defense of the existing order. Nisbet says, in effect,
that we can have the feeling of community without actually
creating communities. Similarly, President Reagan loved to use
John Winthrop's image of a city upon a hill to describe a huge
nation that is, no matter what its virtues, nearly the antithesis
of Winthrop's radically communitarian ideal. President Bush
mystically calls for "a thousand points of light," an expression
that seems to be simply a way of articulating certain public
concerns without having to make changes or to pay for them.

Volunteerism is not a sufficient remedy for America's
ills. Meaningful participation must be connected with power.
The collectivity in which one is participating must control, to a
large degree, those forces that affect it. Yet, in the face of the
internationalization of power, autonomy has become less of a
possibility for political communities. Dahl writes, "The trouble
with the small city in the modern world is that there are too

14. Robert A. Nisbet, *The Quest for Community* (New York: Oxford University
Press, 1953).
15. Ibid., 74.

many problems it cannot cope with, because they go beyond its boundaries."[16] Dahl raises an extremely important problem, but one that cannot be solved by investing more authority in national and international bodies. Although these governmental units may be given ever greater duties, they will be ineffectual because of power's very nature.

All power rests ultimately on the consent of the governed.[17] Even the most totalitarian government cannot always use coercion to exercise its will. Large governments, distant from the actual lives of their subjects, notoriously find it difficult to attain more than a grudging acceptance of their laws. In contrast, smaller countries with democratic governments, like ancient Athens or the American colonies at the time of our revolution, can generate surprising amounts of power because they have been able to count on the active support of their citizens. In short, the creation of large, nonparticipatory governments might not increase power; and small, democratic governments should not inevitably be associated with weakness, for their ability to command allegiance and active participation is itself a formidable source of power.

Then put the power question aside, say democracy's critics, and face the fact that if people were to attain power they would not know what to do with it. The political and economic worlds have grown too complicated for ordinary people to rule themselves directly. Perhaps in a simpler world direct democracy made sense, but now ordinary people simply lack sufficient intellect and awareness to make good decisions, and their outlooks are too parochial. Ordinary people may or may not be capable of responsibly choosing their representatives, but they cannot govern themselves directly.

I do not want to romanticize the political capabilities of the average person, yet neither should they be underestimated. My own ideas about democracy and human nature are shaped

16. Dahl, "The City," 958.
17. See Hannah Arendt, "What Is Authority?", in *Between Past and Future* (New York: Penguin Books, 1954), 91–142.

by my two years as a community organizer in Texas and Arkansas. In Jonesboro, Arkansas, I spent a lot of time with poor people who lacked the benefits of a college or, often, even a high school education. At least one kind and generous member of the group was illiterate. Whenever I write about democracy, I think about those members taking power. Could they wield power responsibly and make intelligent decisions about public matters? I believe that they could, and with a little practice, would so splendidly—certainly at least as well as the educated elite that now governs in their name. I am not saying that there are no qualifications for holding power in a democracy; I am saying that ordinary people active in religious and community organizations have those qualifications.

The politics of democracy is based on a respect for the limited abilities of citizens to think abstractly and to care about what is distant from their everyday lives. The Antifederalists sought to keep power local so that it would remain within the purview of the citizens. The lesson is that people are capable of self-rule when institutions are drawn to human scale. Conversely, according to Aristotle, human beings are incapable of making good laws for a vast territory because a large state will inevitably encompass many different cultures; citizens, whose knowledge does not extend much beyond their experience, cannot legislate for those who are very different from themselves.[18] According to this theory, even an emperor had either to permit a nation he had conquered to govern itself or else force it to become like his own country so that he could understand it.

In order to refute Aristotle's teachings on human political capacity, advocates of centralization had either to dispute his characterization of political knowledge and say that familiarity with the locale being ruled was not one of its central components or else discover a way to make politics less dependent on

18. *The Politics*, ed. and trans. Ernest Barker (New York: Oxford University Press, 1958), 105, par. 14.

the citizens. The Federalists did both: they said that custom and experience did not yield reliable political knowledge, and they separated power from the citizenry by expanding the nation and by creating a set of political and economic institutions in which only a few could actively participate. The Federalists said that ordinary people are not capable of direct self-rule and that direct democracy conflicts with higher goals such as maximizing national power and protecting property, and other individual rights, from encroachment by the majority.

This book explores the nature of democracy. In chapter 2 I will argue that although the Puritans are thought to be authoritarian elitists, their system of church government was actually decentralist. The Puritans believed in hierarchy, but in crucial respects they were democratic. In chapter 3 I will show that pre-Revolutionary American radicalism had as much to do with participation and community as it did with individual rights. And although Antifederalist political thought has been frequently denigrated as confused liberalism, in chapter 4 I will make the case that it is more accurately described as conservative democracy; that is, elements of Antifederalist thought have more in common with the theories of Burke and Hume than they do with those of Locke, Jefferson, and Paine. In chapter 5, I will show that Hamilton and Madison shared the Antifederalist belief that human beings are essentially localist and parochial, and therefore they thought it would be difficult for the large, centralized, national government they proposed to win the affections of the people. To overcome this problem, the Federalists developed the doctrine of popular sovereignty. In the final chapter I will try to describe more precisely the legacy of early American politics for our own time.

Americans are deeply divided about democracy, but they are also confused about its character. They have been taught by their most prominent political teachers that what they most valued in democracy could be found in a liberal regime. Americans have learned that what is good in their tradition is liberal, and much of what was bad was radical or direct democracy. In this essay I hope to clarify both the meaning of democracy and its place in the American political tradition. By so doing, I intend to give democracy's critics a clearer target and democracy's supporters something to think about.

2

Direct Democracy and the Puritan Theory of Membership

lthough it appears to be one of the most elitist elements of their political thought, the establishment by the Puritans of strict standards for membership in town and church was, in fact, closely related to the most democratic aspects of their political thinking. Because they placed so much power in the hands of the members, the Puritans maintained high standards for membership in Congregational churches. Although the American Puritans are not today perceived as democratic in any sense of the word—in part, because of confusion about the different natures of democracy and liberalism—their attempt to create a localist church structure served as a model for radical democracy in eighteenth-century America.

It is difficult for democratic theorists to coherently reject Puritan criteria for membership and to substitute for them an

ideal of "universal democracy." Such an ideal contradicts the
very nature of democracy. Loyalty to and love for the community, unmistakably Puritan values, preclude a universal democracy. The inherent relation of democracy to public virtue, the
need for citizens to value the public good over private interests,
forces a community to attend to the character of the members
and to the criteria for membership.

Political scientists have not paid much attention to the
American Puritans.[1] Few textbooks in American politics even
mention them. Most Puritan scholarship has come from students of history, religion, and English literature.[2] As a result,
the contribution of the Puritans to a living tradition of American political theory has not been fully recognized. Nevertheless,
the political ideas and practices of the Puritans should be of
interest to social scientists, political theorists in particular, and
to political actors who seek to revive direct democracy. The
Puritan effort to create a localist church structure should serve
as an instructive example for those who today seek to decen-

1. The most important exception is Wilson Carey McWilliams, *The Idea of
Fraternity in America* (Berkeley: University of California Press, 1973). Perhaps someday
John H. Schaar will publish his great lectures on John Winthrop. In his examination of
the Puritans, Schaar is particularly interested in the relationship of authority and
community. He takes up those themes in several essays in *Legitimacy in the Modern State*
(New Brunswick, N.J.: Transaction Press, 1981), including the title essay, "The Case
for Patriotism," and "The Use of Literature for the Study of Politics: The Case of
Benito Cereno."

2. I do not mean to imply that the others have not made a significant
contribution to understanding American politics and political thought. Students of
politics can greatly profit from Ralph Barton Perry's *Puritanism and Democracy* (New
York: Vanguard, 1944). Among his many essential works on American Puritanism, the
late Perry Miller, a professor of English at Harvard, published *The New England Mind:
The Seventeenth Century* (Cambridge: Harvard University Press, 1982 [1939]). His
Orthodoxy in Massachusetts (Cambridge: Harvard University Press, 1933) takes up
explicitly political themes. Sacvan Bercovitch, also a professor of English at Harvard,
is the author of *The Puritan Origins of the American Self* (New Haven: Yale University
Press, 1975) and *The American Jeremiad* (Madison: University of Wisconsin Press, 1978).
Important works by historians include Stephen Foster's *Their Solitary Way* (New Haven:
Yale University Press, 1971) and Darrett B. Rutman's *Winthrop's Boston* (New York:
W. W. Norton, 1965). The politics of the English Puritans has been far more extensively
explored. Current bibliographies appear in A. S. P. Woodhouse, ed., *Puritanism and
Liberty* (London: Dent, Everyman Press, 1986 [1938]), and David Wootton, ed., *Divine
Right and Democracy* (New York: Penguin Books, 1987).

tralize power. As repellent as some of their ideas and practices may seem, the Puritans made an important contribution to the indigenous democratic tradition in American political thought.

I

The most recent scholarship on the Puritans has sought to correct an unduly secular interpretation of the Puritan mission in the classic work of Perry Miller by stressing the theological purposes and vocabulary of Puritan theory.[3] Although a truer picture of Puritan religious practices may emerge from these studies, the political aims of the Puritans are in danger of being overlooked. Contemporary students of the Puritans may have lost the balance attained by Tocqueville's assertion that "Puritanism was not merely a religious doctrine, but it corresponded in many points with the most absolute democratic and republican theories."[4] If either the religious or the political element is unduly stressed, a false picture of the New England Puritans emerges.

Although the Puritans were deeply Christian, they were not primarily academic theologians; their theology was profoundly political, and their religious thought was infused with such concepts as power, participation, and autonomy. Both town and church were taken to be small polities. According to leading Puritan theologian Thomas Hooker, the church was "a

3. See Patricia Caldwell, *The Puritan Conversion Narrative* (New York: Cambridge University Press, 1983); John S. Coolidge, *The Pauline Renaissance in England* (New York: Oxford University Press, 1970); C. L. Cohen, *God's Caress* (New York: Oxford University Press, 1986); Patrick Collinson, *Godly People* (London, England: Hambledon, 1987); David D. Hall, "On Common Ground: The Coherence of American Puritan Studies," *William and Mary Quarterly*, 3d ser., 44 (1987): 193–229.

4. Alexis de Tocqueville, *Democracy in America*, 2 vols., trans. Henry Reeve (New York: Schocken, 1961), 1:19.

visible politick body."[5] The blurring of religion and politics can be seen further in the fact that the Puritans did not sharply distinguish the principles of membership in church and town. The members of both bodies were joined by a covenant, and both towns and churches claimed the right to exclude those whom they believed to be morally unfit for membership.[6]

As Tocqueville indicated, several tenets of Puritan religious thought were closely related to direct democracy. These included the principle of autonomy for churches and communities, the identification of churches with their members, the concept of covenant, and popular election of church officers. The Puritan practice of allowing all adult male members of the community and church to vote for their magistrates and clergy made the bodies politic of New England among the most, if not the most, democratic in the world. The principle of local autonomy was embodied in their theory of church organization, and it was also the basis of their struggle with England over the right of self-governance. As Nathaniel Hawthorne wrote, "[The Puritans] looked with most jealous scrutiny to the exercise of power which did not emanate from themselves."[7]

The Puritans criticized the Anglican and Roman Catholic churches for being centralized, hierarchical, and universal: power in those churches issued from the central authority down to local congregations; that authority was made up of ranked church officers (bishops, cardinals, etc.); and everyone in a certain area was either admitted to the church or required to be a member of it. The Puritans, on the other hand, equated the

5. Thomas Hooker, *A Survey of the Summe of Church-Discipline* (New York: Arno Press, 1972 [1648]), 15. All references are to part 1 of this book.

6. The Puritans did not distinguish sharply between membership in the town and in the church. Both town and church were conceived of as small bodies politic created by covenants. See Champlain Burrage, *The Church Covenant Idea: Its Origins and Development* (Philadelphia: American Baptist Publications, 1904), chap. 7.

7. Nathaniel Hawthorne, "My Kinsman, Major Molineux," in *Young Goodman Brown and Other Tales*, ed. Brian Harding (New York: Oxford University Press, 1987), 37. See also John Winthrop, *Winthrop's Journal*, 2 vols., ed. J. K. Hosmer (New York: Charles Scribner's Sons, 1908), 2:24.

church with the body of Christ; to admit everyone, even open and unrepentant sinners, to the church was to pollute Christ's body.[8]

In England the Puritan criticism of the established church remained theoretical; in New England the Puritans developed an alternative structure of small, autonomous churches in which the membership, not the church officers, had sovereign authority. To be a member of a Congregational church, said Hooker, allows one to choose the officers of the congregation.[9] "Every man hath right," said Hooker, "to meddle with the Congregation whereof he is a member."[10]

The Puritans believed that the model for their church system could be found in the New Testament. In his treatise "The Ways of Congregational Churches Cleared," New England Minister John Cotton claimed that the Christian churches in the second century A.D. were "almost" democratic and certainly congregational. In one key passage he links the primitive church with democracy:

> [I]f a man search the approved authors of this age, he shall see the form of the government, to be almost like to a democracy: for every single church had equal power of preaching the word, administering sacraments, excommunicating heretics and notorious offenders, absolving penitents, choosing, calling, ordaining ministers, and upon just and weighty causes deposing them again: power also of gathering conventions and synods, etc.[11]

Cotton did not fully embrace the principle of democracy because the Puritan system of church governance was not based

8. Hooker, *Survey*, 15. See also Winthrop, *Journal*, 1:282; Edmund S. Morgan, *Visible Saints* (Ithaca: Cornell University Press, 1963); and Miller, *Orthodoxy*, 77, 85.

9. Hooker, *Survey*, 64. See also Winthrop, *Journal*, 1:110.

10. Hooker, *Survey*, 65.

11. Larzer Ziff, ed., *John Cotton on the Churches of New England* (Cambridge: Harvard University Press, 1968), 297.

on equality of membership. Although in one sense all of those chosen for salvation were equal in the eyes of God, the Puritans divided the community into high and low, elders and brethren, magistrates and citizens, church officers and laity, and then sought to unite them all. The Congregational church was made up of members called brethren, elders, deacons, a minister, and a teacher. In their introduction to Cotton's essay *Keys to the Kingdom of Heaven*, English Puritans Thomas Goodwin and Philip Nye wrote:

> In commonwealths, it is a dispersion of several portions of power and rights into several hands, jointly to concur and agree in acts and process of weight and moment, which causeth that healthful [mixture] and constitution of them, which makes them lasting and preserves their peace, but none of all sorts find they are excluded, but as they have a share of concernment, so that a fit measure of power or privilege is left and betrusted them.[12]

Lack of equality between elders and brethren did not mean that power was restricted to those on top of the social scale; all members were given a share of power, privilege, and authority. The assent of both elders and brethren were needed for a church to take collective action.[13] The brethren elected the church officers, including the minister.[14] The Cambridge Platform of 1648 said that the powers of the church members included not only the election of officers but also the admission and removal of members and the right to bring a dispute between officers and members to the whole body.[15]

 The town government paralleled that of the church. In

---

12. Ibid., 73.
13. Ibid., 80.
14. Ziff, *John Cotton*, 80. See also Hooker, *Survey*, 9, and Morgan, *Visible Saints*, 11, 28.
15. Williston Walker, ed., *The Creeds and Platforms of Congregationalism* (Boston: Pilgrim Press, 1960 [1893]), 218.

fact, in the early days of the Massachusetts Bay Colony, church and town governments were virtually indistinguishable.[16] From 1631 to 1634 all members of the Massachusetts company were members of the General Court, which met once a year.[17] Day-to-day governing was done by assistants, who were elected by the freemen, and by the governor and deputy governor, who were elected by the assistants. This arrangement was approved by the Massachusetts freemen during the first General Court.[18] Later, in 1634, the governing system moved away from direct democracy and toward representation: a group of deputies elected by the people was added to the ruling body.[19]

The element of hierarchical authority in the Puritan scheme of town and church governments cannot be denied. Although the members elected their officers, the Cambridge Platform states that the everyday governing of the church is to be left to the elders. The members should submit to the elders unless there is "sufficient and weighty cause" for disobedience.[20] The people have the right to choose their magistrates, said Winthrop, but once they have done so, they must obey as if the magistrate's voice were that of God.[21] Winthrop wrote:

> [W]hen the people have chosen men to be their rulers, and to make their laws, and bound themselves by oath to submit thereto, now to combine together (a lesser part of them) in a public petition to have any order repealed, which is not repugnant to the law of God, savors of resisting an order of God; for the people, having deputed others, have no power to make or alter laws, but are to be subject.[22]

16. Rutman, *Winthrop's Boston*, 62, 65.
17. Winthrop, *Journal*, 1:63, note 4, and 74.
18. Ibid., 1:75, note 1.
19. Ibid., 1:122–25.
20. Walker, *Creeds and Platforms*, 219.
21. Winthrop, *Journal*, 1:303.
22. Ibid.

Winthrop tried to sustain the tension between active popular participation in decision making and the preservation of authority. This was not easy to do, and his journal is full of instances of the people seeking more power. For example, when it was rumored that some magistrates wanted to appoint governors for life, the people demanded, and won their demand, that the principle of annual elections be publicly reaffirmed.[23]

These demands on the part of the people should not be taken simply as signs that the Puritan government was authoritarian. The Puritan experiment itself taught the people that they legitimately possessed a share of power. When the people sought more control, they were emphasizing half of the Puritan ideal; in stressing the necessity for submission to authority, Winthrop emphasized the other half. The Puritan political system was thus different from a political system that forbids the people to become involved in politics. Historian Stephen Foster wrote:

> Puritan doctrine itself tended to contradict its own social ideal. Advocates of political hierarchy would do well to base their franchise on something other than church membership; governors who rule by God's ordinance should not make their offices dependent on popular elections. . . . [A]bove all, anyone who maintains traditional concepts of social relationships should not found them on voluntary contracts. . . . Though it sounds strange to say it, few societies in Western culture have ever depended more thoroughly or more self-consciously on the consent of their members than the allegedly repressive "theocracies" of early New England.[24]

The Puritan political outlook cannot accurately be described as liberal. They did not believe in privacy or individual

23. Ibid., 1:302–5. See also 1:79, 133, 143, 323.
24. *Their Solitary Way*, 7, 156. See also Perry, *Puritanism and Democracy*, 107; and Ziff, *John Cotton*, 18, 28–29, 58.

rights such as freedom of speech. On or about 14 June 1631 a servant, Philip Ratcliff, "being convict . . . of most foul, scandalous invectives against our churches and government, was censured to be whipped, lose his ears, and be banished the plantation, which was presently executed."[25] Later in the year "a young fellow was whipped for soliciting an Indian squaw to incontinency. Her husband and she complained of the wrong, and were present at the execution, and very well satisfied."[26] At the same court one Henry Linne was whipped and banished for criticizing ("slandering") the colony in letters to England.[27] In 1634 Abigail Gifford was sent back to England for "being found . . . sometimes distracted, and a very burdensome woman."[28]

The Puritan lack of tolerance was, in part, a result of the seriousness with which they took ideas. They believed that their own ideas about the correct form of religious worship were true, and they defined political liberty as the right to put those ideas into practice. They feared that radical dissent which challenged the fundamental principles of Congregationalism would divide and destroy their fragile experiment.[29] Although they set limits on dissent, the Puritans publicly discussed the most important religious and political questions facing the community. They did not coerce their opponents before engaging them in debate; Winthrop's *Journal* describes many such dialogues.[30] For example, Winthrop writes, "A proposition was made by the people, that every company of trained men might choose their own captain and officers; but the governor giving them reasons to the contrary, they were satisfied without it."[31] Democracy is impossible without public deliberation; citizens

25. Winthrop, *Journal*, 1:64.
26. Ibid., 1:67.
27. Ibid.
28. Ibid., 1:144, see also 1:147.
29. Winthrop, *Journal*, 1:239. See also Perry Miller, *Roger Williams: His Contribution to the American Tradition* (New York: Atheneum, 1970), 23, and Perry, *Puritanism and Democracy*, 97.
30. Winthrop, *Journal*, 1:66, 211–18.
31. Ibid., 1:79.

must be able to express their ideas about public matters and to hear various viewpoints on those issues. The Puritans encouraged such public discussion, but they set limits on it that would be intolerable today. Dissenters could persist only until they "were so divided from the rest of the country in their judgment and practice, as it could not stand with the public peace, that they should continue amongst us. So, by the example of Lot in Abraham's family, and after Hagar and Ishmael, he saw they must be sent away."[32]

To say that the Puritan leaders were not liberals does not imply that they were self-consciously democratic. If asked, Cotton and Winthrop might have called their government an elected aristocracy or a mixed government, one that combined monarchical, aristocratic, and democratic components. Winthrop said, "The best part of a community is always the least, and of that best part the wiser is always the lesser."[33] Cotton wrote, "Democracy, I do not conceive that ever God did ordain as a fit government either for church or commonwealth."[34] I am suggesting instead that the Puritans were proto-democrats, that certain elements of their theory and practice were highly democratic and conflicted with, and eventually undermined, those elements in it that were undemocratic.

One reason why the democratic elements in Puritan political thought have not been generally recognized is the frequent conflation of democracy and liberalism. A crucial distinction between liberal and democratic theory is their respective locations of power. In liberal theory, the people transfer their power to representative institutions and thereby authorize the actions of their representatives. The representatives in the liberal state are popularly elected, yet the people do not actively wield power. In a direct democracy, power not only originates in the people but is often exercised by them.

32. Winthrop, *Journal*, 1:257. See also 1:286, 328–29. For one of many extensive open debates about public matters, see Winthrop, *Journal*, 1:211–18.
33. Ibid., 2:121.
34. Winthrop, *Journal*, 1:125, note 1. See also *John Cotton*, 27.

The differing locations of power in liberal and democratic political thought have led to divergent theoretical preoccupations. Although liberalism possesses a theory of human nature, its primary concern is with the world external to human beings. Political theorist John Schaar suggests that liberal thought "teaches us to see the political world existing 'out there'—external to ourselves, given, somehow objective and constituted by its own laws."[35] By comparison, it may be said that, whatever its interest in institutions, democratic political thought focuses its attention on the citizens. Issues of education, friendship, virtue, and patriotism are at the heart of democratic thought. Because the citizens wield the power in a democracy, their character is of crucial concern to the community.

Democrats are forced to consider the question that divided national from congregational churches: should all the residents of a particular area necessarily be included in the citizenry?[36] Should all those who seek to join the polity, regardless of their character or purposes, be admitted? Is anyone to be excluded and, if so, upon what grounds? These questions were at the heart of the Puritan theory of membership, and they arose, I believe, not simply from Puritan elitism, but from the willingness of the Puritans to hand over to ordinary people a great deal of power in their churches and communities.

When democracy is properly distinguished from liberalism, the affinity between Puritanism and democracy becomes more apparent.[37] Although they fit neatly into neither category, Puritan theories of town and church membership are closer to democracy than to liberalism.[38] To study the interrelationship

35. *Legitimacy*, 53.
36. Liberals might also address the question of membership. After all, American citizenship at the national level is restricted. But my interest is primarily in face-to-face membership in smaller political bodies such as cities and towns.
37. As I interpret his great work, *Puritanism and Democracy*, Perry blurred the distinction between liberalism and democracy.
38. Puritan leaders used the term "democracy" only in a pejorative sense. See Winthrop, *Journal*, 2:118, 121, 235, and Ziff, *John Cotton*, 27–28.

of Puritanism and direct democracy is to illuminate hidden, albeit problematic, aspects of both.

II

The American Puritans, or Congregationalists, rejected the idea of "membership-in-general" in both town and church. Whereas all Christians and all true (that is, Protestant) churches might be loosely linked in loving brotherhood, a person could only be a member of the particular church and of the political community whose covenant he or she had publicly affirmed. Only in that community could the person become a full citizen, and only that church could offer the sacraments to him or her; similarly, a clergyman could only administer the sacraments to the members of the church that had elected him.

In contrast, Hillaire Belloc has described his pleasure in attending Catholic mass at every town along the path of his pilgrimage to Rome. The Puritan abroad knew no such solace. When John Winthrop's nascent community arrived at Salem on the *Arabella* in 1630, they presented a newborn baby to the Puritan church there for baptism. Because its parents were not in covenant with their church, the Salem minister refused to baptize the baby. Winthrop promptly wrote to John Cotton, an influential minister then living in England, pleading for his condemnation of this unbrotherly act. Cotton acceded because at that point he believed that a church covenant was desirable, but not essential. Soon the Puritans of Massachusetts Bay, including Cotton and Winthrop, converted to Salem's position.[39]

What were the key elements of this system of church

39. Ziff, *John Cotton*, 12, 18, 41; Morgan, *Visible Saints*, 85–87; Winthrop, *Journal*, 1:107; Hooker, *Survey*, 62–63.

organization that so carefully and sharply distinguished between members and nonmembers? An examination of the Puritan theory of church organization is necessary in order to set the context for their ideas concerning the restriction of town and church membership. The essential features of the Puritan theory of church organization and membership included the identification of the church with its members, the restriction of the authority of a church and its clergy to its own members, the idea of covenant, and autonomy afforded to local churches.[40]

In the theory of church organization that came to be called the New England Way, each particular church was identified at once with its covenanted members and, paradoxically, with the body of Christ. "There is no greater church than a *Congregation*," read the Cambridge Platform of 1648, "which may ordinarily meet in one place."[41] The church did not derive its identity from its building or clergy, but from its members. William Ames, one of the theoretical founders of Congregationalism, described a church as a fellowship of faithful believers.[42]

At the heart of this definition of a church was the desire to limit the power of institutions. If a distinction was made between an institution and its membership, the institution could act independently of the membership's will, something the Puritans wished to avoid. In fact, this separation of the church from the members was what the Puritans took to be the Anglican error and the Catholic heresy. The seemingly magnanimous concept of "membership-in-general" implied, to the Puritans, a division between institutions and the members that would produce a centralized power with unlimited capacity for expansion.

40. Ziff, *John Cotton*, 2; Loren Baritz, *City on a Hill* (New York: John Wiley, 1964), 35; R. F. Scholz, "Clerical Consociation in Massachusetts Bay," *William and Mary Quarterly*, 3d ser., 29 (1972):403.

41. Walker, *Creeds and Platforms*, 207. See also Hooker, *Survey*, 45, and A. D. Lindsay, *The Modern Democratic State* (New York: Oxford University Press, 1972 [1943]), 117.

42. William Ames, *The Marrow of Sacred Divinity* (London: 1638), 136–40.

The New England Puritans directly linked the citizen to the bodies politic of church and town, and to God, through covenants.[43] Although their principles were essentially the same, there were actually two covenants, one for the church and one for the town.[44] Donald Lutz writes that the covenant form was repeated throughout New England, parts of the central colonies (including the Dutch colonies), and later in the Southern piedmont. "Wherever dissenting Protestantism went, so too went their church covenants."[45] The covenant expresses the very essence of the Puritan project.[46] "Mutual covenanting and confederating of the Saints in the fellowship of the faith according to the order of the Gospel, is that which gives Constitution and being to a visible church," wrote Thomas Hooker.[47]

The covenant consisted of a set of mutually binding promises to love one another and to obey the laws of Christ.[48] The original covenant of the Charlestown–Boston church said:

> Wee whose names are hereunder written, being by His most wise, & good Providence brought together in this part of America in the Bay of Massachusetts, & desirous to unite our selves into one Congregation, or Church, under the Lord Jesus Christ our Head, in such sort as becometh all those whom He hath Redeemed, & Sanctifyed to Himselfe, do hereby solmnly, and religiously . . . Promisse, & bind orselves, to walke in our wayes according to the Rule of the Gospell, & in all sincere Conformity to his holy Ordinaunces, & in mutuall love,

43. Donald S. Lutz, "From Covenant to Constitution in American Political Thought," *Publius* 10 (1980): 101–33; Ames, *Marrow*, 140–41; Hooker, *Survey*, 45.

44. Miller, *Roger Williams*, 37.

45. *The Origins of American Constitutionalism* (Baton Rouge: Louisiana State University Press, 1988), 25.

46. Ziff, *John Cotton*, 41–68; Ames, *Marrow*, 140–41.

47. Hooker, *Survey*, 46.

48. Lutz, *Origins*, 17–27.

and respect each to other, so neere as God shall give us grace.[49]

Because it was an actual document, sworn and signed by each member, the covenant unified members differently than did the fictional social contract described in liberal political theory. Whereas the Lockean contract recognized boundaries on individual freedom of will and movement in order to retain rights of property and security, the Puritan covenant made no mention of individual rights.[50] The liberal social contract, according to Hanna Pitkin, justified the tacit, passive consent of the citizens to the actions of the government.[51] The covenant went beyond consent.[52] To subscribe to the covenant was an act that created a body politic and thus changed the relationships among those subscribing to it.[53] The members had been isolated individuals; they were now openly declared brothers and sisters. Subscription to the covenant was a voluntary act that indicated that the new member understood and embraced the principles and goals of the community before binding himself or herself to it. Hooker said, "There can be no necessary tye of mutual accord and fellowship come, but by free engagement, free (I say) in regard of any human constraint."[54] The covenant, Hooker continued, is

> that cement which soders them all, that *soul* as it were, that acts all the parts and particular persons so interested

49. Walker, *Creeds and Platforms*, 131. See also Baritz, *City on a Hill*, 13; Kenneth Lockridge, *A New England Town* (New York: W. W. Norton, 1970), 4–5; and Lutz, *Origins*, 25.

50. See Sheldon S. Wolin, "Contract and Birthright," in *The New Populism*, ed. Harry Boyte and Frank Riessman (Philadelphia: Temple University Press, 1986); Richard H. Niebuhr, "The Idea of Covenant and American Democracy," *Church History* 23 (1954): 126–35; Lutz, "From Covenant to Constitution"; Miller, *The New England Mind*, 398–462; and Cohen, *God's Caress*.

51. Hanna Fenichel Pitkin, "Obligation and Consent, I," *American Political Science Review* 59 (1965): 990–99.

52. Lutz, *Origins*, 17.

53. Hooker, *Survey*, 46.

54. Ibid., 47.

in such a way, for there is no man constrained to enter such a condition, unless he will: and he that will enter, must also willingly bind and engage himself to each member of society to promote the good of the whole, or else a member actually he is not.[55]

There is much to praise in the covenant as a model of creating political bodies, particularly its emphasis on individual will and choice. On the other hand, it must be noted that the covenant sharply distinguishes between those inside and those outside of it, and therefore it is difficult for those on the inside not to feel superior to those on the outside.[56] In contrast, Roger Williams, for example, in most ways an orthodox Puritan, rejected the idea that God had a covenant with any community since the one with ancient Israel, and for that reason he was the Puritan most tolerant of other religions and cultures, particularly that of the Indians.[57]

Each covenanted church was seen by the Puritans as a small, self-governing body politic. Hooker said, "We deny that Christ hath given power of jurisdiction to one particular congregation over another."[58] Winthrop, writing in his journal, said, "[N]o church or person can have power over another church."[59] The one central authority among the local churches was the synod, comprised of ministers from the various churches in a given area.[60] The synod met to discuss problematic questions of common concern, such as theological controversies and issues of church organization.[61] In their preface to Cotton's *The Keys to the Kingdom of Heaven*, English Puritan theorists Thomas Goodwin and Philip Nye described the purpose of the synods

55. Ibid., 50.
56. See Bercovitch, *The American Jeremiad.*
57. Miller, *Roger Williams*, 52, 183, and passim.
58. Hooker, *Survey*, 65.
59. Winthrop, *Journal*, 1:113.
60. Ziff, *John Cotton*, 2; Baritz, *City on a Hill*, 35; Scholz, "Clerical Consociation," 403.
61. Rutman, *Winthrop's Boston*, 132–33.

and the limits upon their power: "And because these particular congregations, both elders and people, may disagree and miscarry, and abuse this power committed to them; he [Christ] therefore . . . asserteth an association or communion of churches, sending their elders and messengers into a synod."[62] The aim of the synod was "rectifying maladministration and healing dissention in particular congregations, and the like cases."[63] When a controversy of faith "disturbed the peace of particular congregations," or when a particular case became too troublesome for a single church to handle, then it should be brought to a synod.[64]

Immediately after describing the powers of the synods, Goodwin and Nye carefully stated the limits on their power. Synods could only discern matters of fact and censure a particular church or party. They could not excommunicate a member or a congregation and could only withdraw communion from that church. The synod's power was circumscribed by the principle of local autonomy, a principle sanctioned by the authority of Christ.[65]

> And also for the extent of this power in such assemblies and association of churches, he limits and confines that also unto cases, and with cautions . . . to wit, they . . . should not entrench or impair the privilege of entire jurisdiction committed unto each congregation (as a liberty purchased them by Christ's blood) but leave them free to the exercise and use thereof, until they abuse that power, or are unable to manage it; and in this case only to assist, guide, and direct them, and not take on them to administer it for them, but with them, and by them.[66]

62. Ziff, *John Cotton*, 75.
63. Ibid., 76.
64. Ibid.
65. The synod system influenced the design of the first New England Confederation, which was founded in 1643. This confederation sought to achieve only limited purposes and guaranteed autonomy to each member. See Winthrop, *Journal*, 2:100–101.
66. Ziff, *John Cotton*, 75–76.

In other words, at least in theory, the synods lacked the power to interfere regularly with the affairs of local congregations.[67] The unity among the churches would not come primarily from a central institution, but from the members who had professed a faith in the teachings of the Old and New Testaments, read by the light of Congregational principles. Unity replaced the Anglican and Catholic ideas of uniformity imposed by a church hierarchy.[68]

The Congregational theory of church organization emerged from the Puritans' desire to limit the power of the church hierarchy in order to prevent the power of church leaders from usurping that of the members and of Christ. I have shown that the Puritans restricted the power of the hierarchy not only by making them subject to election by church members but by defining the church as a particular congregation of covenanted members and by asserting the autonomy of that church. It remains to be examined, however, why the Puritans restricted their membership to those they believed understood the principles of their community and showed that they were capable of carrying out those principles.

III

There was nothing automatic about the process of becoming a member of a Puritan church or community. The fact that

67. The synods became more powerful as Puritanism declined. See Scholz, "Clerical Consociation," 406. The rise of the synods was a deviation from the Congregationalist principle of local autonomy. Perry, however, suggests an interesting line of inquiry when he writes that "There was . . . an inherent conflict between the idea of the single church as an autonomous group of believers and the idea that there was one authentic polity and doctrine which was prescribed for all churches" (*Puritanism and Democracy*, 110).

68. R. H. Bainton, *Christian Unity and Religion in New England* (Boston: Beacon Press, 1964), 73. For an opposing view, see Miller, *Orthodoxy*.

individuals moved to town did not necessarily mean, as it does today, that they would be received as members.[69] "It is not habitation in the same Towne," wrote Puritan leader Richard Mather, "that distinguisheth Churches, and Church-members from other men, but their mutuall agreement and combination and joyning themselves together in a holy covenant with God."[70] Cotton stated, "We do not open the doors of our churches so wide as to receive all the inhabitants of a nation, or of every town, into our churches."[71] Turks, atheists, the profane, and "men of strange languages," said Thomas Hooker, could not join a Puritan church.[72] Those who wished to join had to affirm the covenant; in order to sign the covenant they had to demonstrate in their actions and speech that they possessed good characters and were not open sinners.

In addition to the covenant principle, the theological basis for discriminating between those who were worthy and unworthy to join the church was the doctrine of "visible saints." According to Hooker, "Visible Saints only are fit matter appointed by God to make up a visible church of Christ."[73] Following Augustine and Calvin, the Puritans believed that God had chosen some people for salvation and rejected others; those who were saved were the saints. Although no one could infallibly separate the saved from the damned, the Puritans felt obliged to determine who was most likely to be chosen. The "saints" had to convince the community of their election before being admitted to the congregation.

What criteria were to be used to separate the visible saints from the visible sinners? The Puritans employed three interconnected standards of increasing strictness: desire to join, outward deportment, and public confession of grace.[74] In the first days of the Puritan experiment, those who said that they

69. Hooker, *Survey*, 13.
70. Burrage, *The Church Covenant Idea*, 103.
71. Ziff, *John Cotton*, 186.
72. Hooker, *Survey*, 14.
73. Ibid.
74. Morgan, *Visible Saints*.

were willing to sign the covenant were generally accepted as saved. There was surely good reason for thinking so since the journey to America was arduous and the conditions there bleak. While no sure way existed to know whom God had saved, it was generally believed that those who walked in an upright, moral fashion in this world would probably be saved in the next.[75] And although it was in God's power to save them, the irreligious and the profane could probably count on being consigned to hell. Thomas Hooker, the most generous of the New England leaders on the question of church membership, argued that it was absurd to allow visible sinners to become church members.

Not to separate those openly sinning from those who appeared to be righteous would lead to chaos, said Hooker, and to think that an outward sinner could be a saint would lead to "folly and madness."[76]

> For then such who to the judgement of charity are members of the devil, may be conceived members of Christ. Those, who to the eye of reason, are servants to sin, may be servants of righteousness and of Christ: and those, who are under the kingdom of darkness by the rule of reasonable charity, by the same rule, at the same time, they may be judged under the kingdom of light. Those may be counted fit to share in the covenant and the priviledges thereof, as sacraments and church society, who are strangers from the covenant, and without God in the world. All which are absurdities, that common sense will not admit.[77]

Nevertheless, Hooker did not want to be too strict. His goal was not to make the church free of all sin and disagreement. He

75. Ibid., 88–89.
76. Hooker, *Survey*.
77. Ibid., 17.

sought to establish the criterion of "rational charity" for admission to church membership. He did not want to exclude all sinners, but only those who did not repent of their sin.[78] He would admit those who were willing to change, "if they come to see their sin, and to reform their evil ways."[79] One could differ with the others on some points of church doctrine and still be a member.[80] He said, "The church consists of some who are faithful and sincere hearted: some counterfeit and false hearted. Some really good, some really bad, only those who appear so bad and vile should not be accepted."[81]

During the course of the church's development in Massachusetts, the Puritans put increasing emphasis on a third criterion for becoming a church member, a public proclamation of one's conversion experience.[82] Historian Edmund Morgan saw in this development an effort to narrow the distance between the visible and invisible churches.[83] Recent scholars have disputed his contention, arguing that the conversion narratives became formulaic so that just about any believer who sought membership could attain it, and even Morgan concedes that at least until 1636 "all well-behaved inhabitants" in the Puritan community could become church members.[84] No matter how generous the Puritans were in practice, it is important to note that, contrary to the accepted rule in contemporary American localities, the New England Puritans denied membership to some people who sought it and banished others from the community because of antisocial or immoral behavior and

78. Ibid., 24.
79. Ibid., 18.
80. Ibid., 60–61.
81. Ibid., 22.
82. Winthrop, *Journal*, 2:199; Morgan, *Visible Saints*, 89.
83. Morgan, *Visible Saints*, 93.
84. Morgan, *Visible Saints*, 104–5. See also Collinson, *Godly People*, chaps. 1 and 20; Robert Middlekauff, *The Mathers* (New York: Oxford University Press, 1971), 49; Baritz, *City on a Hill*, 13; Rutman, *Winthrop's Boston*, 56; Lockridge, *A New England Town*, 11; Katherine Brown, "Puritan Democracy: A Case Study," *Mississippi Valley Historical Review* 49 (1963): 377–96; Coolidge, *Pauline Renaissance*, 65; Foster, *Their Solitary Way*.

because of serious doctrinal differences stubbornly held and publicly proclaimed. According to the Puritans, because it was formed by the free consent of its members, the community possessed the right to select as new members those who would help the enterprise, or at least would pose no obvious threat to it.[85] Hooker wrote, "[B]ecause the work . . . is of so great a weight" it is essential to "be carefull and watchfull to search sedulously, and labour to be acquainted with each others fitness and sufficiency in judgment."[86] And John Winthrop said, "[I]t is lawful to take knowledge of all men before we receive them. . . . [The desire is] to have none received into any fellowship with it who are likely to disturb the same."[87]

However much one may respect the Puritans, Winthrop's view is troubling. Recalling Socrates, one might assert that a political community needs to be disturbed from time to time, and that some of the most disturbing people are precisely the ones who should be welcomed into the community and protected from a hostile public and defensive leaders. The second generation of Puritans perpetrated great crimes in persecuting those who disturbed them, such as the Quakers and witches, as they tried to enforce increasingly rigid religious beliefs and practices. One reason why today we are repelled by the Puritans and reject their model of town and church membership is that modern society is more generous and respectful of diversity than were the Puritans of New England. To the extent that we are more generous and respectful, we can take pride in progress.

But the Puritans offend us for other reasons, above all because they rejected values and ideas now widely held that deserve to be reconsidered. One of these values, already mentioned above, is mobility, which is too often embraced with

85. Hooker, *Survey*, 54, 56.
86. Ibid., 47.
87. Edmund Morgan, *Puritan Political Ideas* (Indianapolis: Bobbs-Merrill, 1965), 92–93. The issue of exclusion is a lively one today for resident management programs in public housing such as the one led by Bertha Gilkey in St. Louis. The tenants' efforts to exclude drug dealers from the projects has elicited criticism from the local branch of the American Civil Liberties Union.

insufficient regard for the personal and political costs of transience. Another modern idea that requires reexamination is the sharp distinction made in liberal thought between the public and private realms that allows the latter to be concerned with individual character and belief, but not the former. In many aspects of American life, membership in a particular organization or group is restricted to those who apply for it, who are qualified to join, and who believe in the purposes of the collectivity. Most colleges, for example, matriculate only those students who seem to possess the ability and the will to study. And decision-making bodies of public interest organizations, such as the American Civil Liberties Union and the National Association for the Advancement of Colored People, would not long tolerate someone on their board of directors who publicly repudiated the ideas of individual rights or racial equality. Yet, in the public realm, liberals insist that membership in communities cannot be restricted according to criteria based on the speech or ideas of the members, no matter how much those members affront or even repudiate the ideals of the community.[88]

Unlike modern liberals, the Puritans attributed to the public realm a sense of purpose and mission that required the active support of its citizens. Government, to the Puritans, was not a set of institutions whose purpose was merely to protect individuals in their persons, property, and rights.[89] Rather than viewing politics as a means to make the world stable enough to allow individuals to pursue their private aims, the Puritans believed that civil and religious communities were formed to attain communal and personal redemption and to serve as

88. Given the fact that most communities in America are not based upon covenanted membership, obnoxious speech should generally be tolerated within them. But special communities such as the Amish deserve the power to censure those rare individuals in their midst who, by their behavior or speech, attempt to destroy their community. Whether or not college campuses should attempt to restrict "hate speech" directed at gays, women, African-Americans, Jews, and other groups is not for me an easily resolvable question.

89. For a Puritan theory of a more constricted public sphere, see Roger Williams in Morgan, *Puritan Political Ideas*, 203–13.

models for others.[90] To be permitted to be a member of such a self-governing community was, for the Puritans, the essence of genuine liberty. In contrast to "natural liberty" or unrestricted freedom, Winthrop called this type of liberty "civil," "federal," or "moral, in reference to the covenant between God and man, in the moral law, and the political covenants and constitutions, amongst men themselves."[91] This rich conception of the public realm led the Puritans to think differently about the standards for membership in the community. In his speech entitled "A Model of Christian Charity," delivered during the voyage from England to America in 1630, John Winthrop linked the mission of the colony with the actions of the community members:

> Now the only way to avoid this shipwreck and to provide for our posterity is . . . to do justly, to love mercy, to walk humbly with our God. For this end, we must be knit together in this work as one man; we must entertain each other in brotherly affection; we must be willing to abridge ourselves of our superfluities, for the supply of others' necessities . . . always having before our eyes our commission and community in the work, our community as members of the same body.[92]

It might be argued that the Puritans were not the last figures in the tradition of American political thought either to link the public realm with the highest ideals or to tie the achievement of those ideals to the will and character of the citizenry.[93] For example, Alexander Hamilton wrote:

> It has been frequently remarked that it seems to have been reserved to the people of this country, by their

90. In Morgan, *Puritan Political Ideas*, 75–93.
91. Perry Miller and Thomas Johnson, eds., *The Puritans: A Sourcebook of Their Writings*, 2 vols. (New York: Harper and Row, 1963), 1:206–7.
92. Morgan, *Puritan Political Ideas*, 92–93.
93. Bercovitch in *American Jeremiad* develops the theme of the city upon a hill as a paradigm for national chauvinism in subsequent American political thought.

conduct and example, to decide the important question, whether societies of men are really capable or not of establishing good government from reflection and choice, or whether they are forever destined to depend for their political constitutions on accident and force.[94]

Both Hamilton and Winthrop tell Americans that their proposed societies have momentous consequences for freedom, since the whole world is watching. But the nature of the Puritan and the Federalist visions are quite different: one seeks to create a community, the other to establish a nation and empire; one is rooted in a radical, decentralist religious ideal, the other in liberal theory.

The crucial difference between the words of Winthrop and those of Hamilton is the place of the people in the polity to be established by the founding. For Winthrop, the character and behavior of the members, their ability to "do justly, to love mercy," are essential to the fortunate outcome of the enterprise. Hamilton also links the "conduct and example" of the people to the success of the American experiment, but only in order for them to ratify a constitution that will largely exclude them from directly wielding power. Hamilton invokes a new "science of politics" that has discovered a method for stabilizing the government regardless of the character of the citizenry.[95] By contrast, Puritan theory made a much more direct and personal connection between the public good and the decisions of the membership. John Winthrop wrote, "This whole adventure growes upon the joynt confidence we have in each others fidelity and resolucion herein, such as no man of us would have ventured it without the reassurance of the rest."[96] Unlike the form of society suggested by Hamilton's political vision, in which the people are relieved of the responsibility of their own gover-

94. No. 1 in *The Federalist*, ed. Jacob E. Cooke (Middletown, Conn.: Wesleyan University Press, 1961), 3.
95. Ibid., no. 9, 51.
96. Quoted in Baritz, *City on a Hill*, 18.

nance by creating a constitution, the very makeup of Puritan government necessitated the continued participation of its members.

The Puritans restricted their membership to those who publicly proclaimed that they supported the principles of the community. Although there are legitimate reasons for democrats today to criticize the Puritan viewpoint, they should also examine the coherence of their own position. The Puritan concern with the criteria for admission to community membership emerged largely from their conception of the public realm as a cause whose success required the active engagement of the citizenry. Radical democrats today also see political community as a cause. The massive decentralization of power called for by contemporary democrats would require communitarian experiments like those undertaken by the Puritans; decentralization would devolve upon the citizens a great deal of power. On what grounds could a revived democracy be less restrictive than the Puritan community in admitting new members?[97]

IV

Traditionally, democracies have been more exclusive than large, centralized governments. Yet some contemporary democrats have called for a "universal democracy," one that would not sharply discriminate between citizens and noncitizens. For example, political theorist Mary G. Dietz writes, "All too often, self-proclaimed populists and 'patriots' exhibit the dark side of collective bonds of association when they exclude, exploit, or harass those deemed unworthy of or unsuitable for inclusion in

97. On the potentially repressive aspects of direct democracy, see William Connolly, *Politics and Ambiguity* (Madison: University of Wisconsin Press, 1987), 3–16.

the community."[98] Another of the most insightful universal democrats is Charles Douglas Lummis, who writes: "Athenian democracy, to which we owe so much, was a democracy among the masters. . . . In a world in which we do not know how to establish democracy universally, it is a time-honored strategy to establish it partially by surrounding it with a wall of discrimination."[99] Lummis argues that democracy must become universal because "the myths and self-deceptions" on which exclusions used to be made have been "exploded."[100] Lummis clearly believes that the ancient connection between democracy and exclusivity can be severed today. But who would be admitted to membership in Lummis's democracy? Everyone who wants to join? Fair enough, but what about the people who do not want to join? What would happen to those who want to remain in or enter the community, but who do not wish to become citizens?

As attractive and generous as Lummis's vision is, the very nature of democracy, even as Lummis himself defines it, seems to make "universal democracy" impossible. Admittedly, because democracy implies equality, there would seem to be little basis for treating any residents or outsiders as less worthy than the citizens; all should be admitted and given equal power. And yet one of the characteristics that Lummis identifies as essential to democracy seems to preclude "universal democracy." Democracy, according to Lummis, requires "political virtue," defined by him as patriotism or love of the community. "Political virtue," Lummis writes, "is the commitment to, knowledge of, and ability to stand for the whole, and is the necessary condition for democracy." Choice of officers by lot,

98. "Populism, Patriotism and the Need for Roots," in *The New Populism*, 269. See also Elizabeth Mensch and Alan Freeman, "A Republican Agenda for Hobbesian America," *Florida Law Review* 41:3 (Summer 1989): 581–622. They write that because the United States affects people in other countries, foreigners should not be excluded from voting in American elections (609).

99. Charles Douglas Lummis, "The Radicalism of Democracy," *democracy* 2 (1982): 9–16.

100. Ibid., 16.

says Lummis, "the symbol of radical democracy, is an expression of trust . . . that no matter who is chosen he . . . will not turn out to be a demagogue, or a political fool, or a knave who will run off with the public funds."[101]

But demagogues, fools, and knaves will inevitably appear, and what should be done about them? The large state in which power has been safely ensconced in distant institutions and then checked and balanced can afford to let the fools prattle; it will arrest the knaves when they go too far. But a democracy, which places virtually all political power in the hands of the citizens, must ask itself: What if some members of the community, or those who wish to join it, do not share its goals or do not care to accept the responsibilities of citizenship? And what should be done if individuals publicly advocate apathy and withdrawal, profit and privacy? What power or place should be given in a democratic community to those who reside in the community, or seek to join it, yet do not believe in democracy and who have shown by their speech and action that they do not desire to exercise power for the common good or are not capable of doing so? I realize that these questions cannot be easily answered, and although I have no ready answers to offer, I am pretty sure that those who call for democracy's revival must address them. Part of what makes the Puritans so interesting and problematic is that they forthrightly took up these painful questions.

In pointing out the link between direct democracy and the Puritan theory of membership, I am not trying to disparage the former or argue for the wholesale adoption of the latter. Nor am I suggesting that the American Puritans were, in fact, democrats. My claims are more modest and tentative. The Puritans of New England developed a set of ideas and practices that influenced radical democrats in early America and that should be studied by those seeking to revive direct democracy today. I have tried to indicate that one element of their political

101. Ibid., 15.

and religious theory, the idea of restricted membership, is more closely related to their proto-democratic character than to their elitism. Or, to put it another way, their elitism resulted in large measure from the amount of power they put in the hands of the citizens.

The theoretical problem of membership in democracies is, I believe, real and difficult. One reason why democratic theorists often avoid the issue is that they are constrained by a liberal vocabulary that insists that all human beings have equal power by virtue of their birth, and not as a result of their commitments. This view is easier to hold when most power is invested in institutions rather than wielded by ordinary human beings. Suffrage may be universal, but the voters have little power. There is no need to be more restrictive in admitting members to America's towns and cities so long as ordinary people do not run them. But if a devolution of power were to begin, we would have to think as much about the character of the citizens as we do now about the qualifications of representatives and the design of political and economic institutions.

3

Democratic Political Culture in the Eighteenth Century

he Puritans' religious vocabulary of localism was largely superseded in the eighteenth and nineteenth centuries by the liberal language of contract and individual rights.[1] This shift of vocabulary occurred gradually and incompletely. Seventeenth-century religious conceptions, practices, and institutions embodying localism were, to a large extent, retained in secular and democratic forms by Americans of the next century. Eventually, after the Civil War, America's predominant values became individualism, competition, expansion, and nationalism; but before these ideals supplanted democracy and community, there oc-

1. The idea of a mainstream political vocabulary in struggle with an alternative one can be found in John H. Schaar, "The Uses of Literature for the Study of Politics: The Case of *Benito Cereno*," in *Legitimacy in the Modern State* (New Brunswick, N.J.: Transaction Press, 1981), 53–88.

curred in revolutionary America a remarkable democratic moment, when popular participation was widespread and radically
democratic ideas were given institutional form.[2]

No longer accepting their status as a colony, Americans
in the middle of the eighteenth century made a revolution to
become an independent body politic.[3] Two sets of colonists
made the Revolution, both of whom might be called Whigs.
One group was radically democratic; the other, fairly moderate,
even conservative.[4] The latter group fought against England in
order to protect, first, their traditional rights as Englishmen
and, later, their natural rights as human beings.[5] From the
standpoint of moderate Whigs, the British subverted the just
order.[6] That just order, not anarchy nor direct democracy, was
necessary to protect natural rights. The whole point, even of
resistance and revolution, was to attain order.[7] The Whig tradition set limits on rebellion: good leaders had to be obeyed, and
revolution could not legitimately overthrow an adequate government.[8] After the war, conservative leaders like Alexander
Hamilton, John Adams, and George Washington sought to curb
the revolutionary spirit they themselves had stirred up among

2. For a detailed historical description of the politics of this period, see E. P.
Douglass, *Rebels and Democrats: The Struggle for Equal Political Rights and Majority Rule
During the Revolution* (Chapel Hill: University of North Carolina Press, 1955); Pauline
Maier, *From Resistance to Revolution* (New York: Vintage, 1974); Merrill Jensen, *The
Articles of Confederation* (Madison: University of Wisconsin Press, 1959); and Jackson
Turner Main, *Political Parties Before the Constitution* (New York: W. W. Norton, 1974).
The concept of a "democratic moment" was first used by Lawrence Goodwyn in
Democratic Promise: The Populist Movement in America (New York: Oxford University
Press, 1976).

3. Pauline Maier describes the evolving political consciousness of revolutionary
America in *From Resistance to Revolution*.

4. Ibid., 96–136. See also Michael Lienesch, *New Order of the Ages: Time, the
Constitution, and the Making of Modern American Political Thought* (Princeton: Princeton
University Press, 1988), 65–70. Lienesch describes the distinction between conservative
and radical Whigs a bit differently than I do. He says that the "court" or conservative
group sought long-term stability, whereas the "country" or left party wanted periodic
reform through such devices as rotation in office (64).

5. Lienesch, *New Order*, 65.

6. Maier, *From Resistance to Revolution*, 28.

7. Ibid., 42.

8. Ibid., 35.

the people.[9] The conservative rendering of Whig theory can be seen in the description of American political principles by William Whiting, a Massachusetts official. In his 1778 reply to the town of Pittsfield, which had rejected the proposed Massachusetts constitution of 1777 as insufficiently grounded in popular will and compact, Whiting emphasized the most conservative aspects of Whig theory, writing that

> [your leaders] never once informed you of this fundamental and eternal truth, that there is no other way given under heaven among men, whereby you can enjoy and have secured to you, the inestimable blessings of liberty, peace and safety, but by resigning your alienable natural rights into the hands of the community, and submitting to be governed by such laws and rules as may be prescribed by the free representers of the people.[10]

Repeatedly, Whiting urged the people to trade their power to a sovereign government in order to protect a portion of their rights.[11]

Not all colonists were willing to hand over their power to the central government. The revolutionaries of this second group were unwilling to employ one set of principles to make revolution against England and another when designing domestic institutions. Historian Pauline Maier calls these revolutionaries "the outer fringes of the opposition."[12] Elisha P. Douglass, the author of *Rebels and Democrats,* the best history of the early American radical movements, described them as the "humbler rebels . . . less privileged groups within the ranks of the Revolutionary party" (v–vi). These groups were to the left of even the most democratic leaders such as Paine, Jefferson, and Samuel Adams.

9. Lienesch, *New Order,* 67–71.

10. Charles S. Hyneman and Donald S. Lutz, eds., *American Political Writing During the Founding Era, 1760–1805,* 2 vols. (Indianapolis: Liberty Press, 1983), 1:464.

11. Ibid., 1:465–67.

12. *From Resistance to Revolution,* 211.

Some will find it surprising that I do not treat Tom Paine and Thomas Jefferson more extensively in this chapter, for many link them with radical democracy. I do not spend much time on them precisely because they are so familiar, and because they had complicated, ambivalent relations with radical democracy. Jefferson defended Shays' Rebellion, but he also called the *Federalist* "the best commentary on the principles of government, which was ever written."[13] Tom Paine was radically democratic in important ways, but he also embraced a liberalism that undermined direct democracy. Eric Foner writes: "What gave coherence to Paine's social outlook was his complete rejection of the past. . . . [Paine was] strikingly modern in ideas, language and social role. . . . Ironically, Paine's very modernism sometimes cut him off from the popular politics his writing helped to inspire."[14]

It is difficult to adequately describe in a short space, or even to convey the extent of, the activities of the early American democrats with whom I am concerned simply because they did so much. An adequate account requires more than a few pages. But in order to understand the nature of the political culture that the Antifederalists defended and the Federalists sought to subvert, one must have some impression of the range of radically democratic actions, ideas, and principles before and after the American Revolution.

The radicals sought to make their particular states participatory, communitarian, egalitarian, and autonomous.[15] They

13. Letter to James Madison, 18 November 1788, in *The Life and Selected Writings of Thomas Jefferson*, ed. A. Koch and W. Peden (New York: Modern Library, 1944), 452. Richard K. Matthews, in *The Radical Politics of Thomas Jefferson* (Lawrence: University Press of Kansas, 1984), argues that Jefferson's commitment to democracy was unequivocal. My own views on Jefferson are closer to those of Herbert Agar, *Land of the Free* (Boston: Houghton Mifflin, 1935), 38–58.

14. Eric Foner, *Tom Paine and Revolutionary America* (New York: Oxford University Press, 1976), xix–xx.

15. In my effort to achieve narrative unity, I attribute to radical democracy a biographical consistency that was absent at the time. I speak as if one coherent group fought for radical state constitutions, acted in the crowds, and took part in the rebellions of western Massachusetts, western Pennsylvania, and North Carolina. I know that this is not the case. Positions often shifted in early American politics, and some who were "radical" at one period took more conservative stances later, and vice-versa. My point is only that radical democracy in early America appeared in these several forms.

did not want merely to protect individual rights against the encroachments of power, nor did they seek to secure their rights by centralizing power. Instead, their method of ensuring liberty was to distribute power broadly in the new states and nation.

The fundamental aim of their political action, institutional design, and economic program was to preserve their traditional communitarian society. Toward this end the democratic radicals took part in direct action, first against the British and then against the elite in the colonies and states. They tried to make the constitutions in the new states highly democratic, insisting that they be written in popular conventions and ratified by the people. In the name of the Revolutionary principle of self-rule, some sectional groups sought to secede from their parent states and independently join the Confederation. They tried to preserve the Articles of Confederation as the national compact because it guaranteed to each state sovereignty over its own affairs. They sought to develop a political economy based on land banks, paper money, and debtor relief laws. In studying mid-eighteenth-century America, one sees several of democracy's key components: direct action, political and economic institutions, equality, autonomy, and face-to-face community. One gets a better feel for the experience of democracy and the requirements of a genuinely democratic political culture by attending to these early radicals than by studying only abstract expressions of democratic political theory.

I

Direct Action   Mass action was familiar and generally accepted in early America. Such action was thought to be normal under free governments, a manifestation of public spirit.[16] Before the Revolution, crowds comprised largely of citizens from the lower classes were directed by elites to enforce local laws and to resist the British.[17] In protest against self-interested rule by oligarchs in England and in their own colonies, crowds burned their opponents in effigy, disrupted judicial proceedings against debtors and rebels, took over courthouses, and released their comrades from jail.[18] In many instances, crowd activity served as the foundation for subsequent, more organized political activity. For example, the Revolutionary party in Philadelphia in 1776 was made up largely of artisans who had earlier taken part in crowd activity and later had joined the Revolutionary militia.[19]

The North Carolina Regulators engaged in direct action to preserve their traditional way of life.[20] Small property owners had lost their holdings by means of the corrupt county government run by lawyers and merchants.[21] Between 1765 and 1771 the Regulators attempted to remedy such conditions as unequal representation, inequitable distribution of property, rigged elections, oligarchical political control, exorbitant salaries for government officials, and high fees of lawyers whose presence was necessary to battle the merchants in court.[22] Their direct

16. Maier, *From Resistance to Revolution*, 21–23.

17. Ibid., 12. See also Foner, *Tom Paine*, 53–57.

18. Maier, *From Resistance to Revolution*, 57.

19. Foner, *Tom Paine*, 60–117.

20. A. Roger Ekirch, "The North Carolina Regulators on Liberty and Corruption, 1766–1771," *Perspectives in American History* 11 (1977–78): 218, 234. Ekirch also offers a survey of historians' assessments of the Regulators. The Regulators referred to themselves as a "community," said historian Marvin Kay. He said that they combined class consciousness with a democratic political vision: "The Regulators were class-conscious white farmers who attempted to democratize local government in their respective counties and to replace their wealthy and corrupt elected officials who would serve the interests of the farmers and, hence, all the people" ("The North Carolina Regulation, 1766–1776," in *The American Revolution: Explorations in the History of American Radicalism*, ed. Alfred F. Young [DeKalb, Ill.: Northern Illinois University Press], 73). See also James Whittenburg, "Planters, Merchants and Lawyers: Social Change and the Origin of the North Carolina Regulation," *William and Mary Quarterly*, 3d ser., 34 (April 1977): 218, 234.

21. Whittenburg, "Planters, Merchants and Lawyers," 221.

22. Douglass, *Rebels and Democrats*, 71–75.

actions in that effort increased their political consciousness. In seeking a redress of economic and political grievances, they overcame the traditional pattern of lower-class deference to authority and privilege.[23]

To achieve their ends, the Regulators wrote and disseminated pamphlets, refused to pay their taxes, and, after they had exhausted peaceful means, kidnapped local officials. In 1769 they tried to take control of the House Assembly. In September 1770 they rioted and took over the courthouse in Orange County.[24] A recent historian of the Regulators has called the May 1771 Battle of Alamance the "largest single instance of collective violence in colonial America."[25] When the archenemy of the Regulators, Governor Fanning, arrested their leader Herman Husband and Husband's comrade, "700 armed Regulators forced the release of the two without any loss of life or serious damage."[26] The Regulators inspired other radical democrats throughout the country.[27]

In the 1780s yeoman farmers attempted to overthrow the government of Massachusetts in a series of actions that have come to be called Shays' Rebellion.[28] Although Daniel Shays, a captain in the American Revolution, was a leader of the insurrection, he was not the only, or even the primary, leader of it.[29] In fact, leadership of the rebellion was, appropriately, nonhierarchical and diffuse.[30] Most of the participants in the Shays movement were Congregationalists; their symbol was a sprig of green.[31] According to historian David Szatmary, Shaysist

23. See "Petition of a Frontier County" in Samuel Eliot Morison, ed., *Sources and Documents Illustrating the American Revolution, 1764–1788 and the Formation of the Federal Constitution,* 2d ed. (New York: Oxford University Press, 1972 [1923]), 83–87.

24. Douglass, *Rebels and Democrats,* 92.

25. Ekirch, "North Carolina Regulators," 199.

26. Ibid., 201.

27. Maier, *From Resistance to Revolution,* 196–97.

28. This account is taken from David P. Szatmary, *Shays' Rebellion: The Making of an Agrarian Insurrection* (Amherst: University of Massachusetts Press, 1980).

29. Ibid., 64.

30. Ibid., 64, 99.

31. Ibid., 60–61, 69.

activity proceeded in three stages: peaceful protest, direct action, and revolution. Between 1784 and 1787 farmers in Massachusetts and other New England states petitioned their state governments for relief from prosecutions of debtors. Protest then took the form of county conventions.[32] When these actions brought little response from state leaders, the farmers gathered into violent crowds, which attacked tax collectors and other targets.[33] In late 1786 Shaysite leaders called for more militant action, like the food riot that had recently occurred in Rhode Island.[34] A large number of farmers responded to the call, and in August 1786 nearly fifteen hundred farmers stopped the proceedings of the Common Pleas Court in Northampton. In September 1786 a number of similar assaults were carried out by groups of three to eight hundred farmers.[35] From 25 to 28 September fifteen hundred Shaysites occupied the Springfield courthouse. By 1787 uprisings involving nearly nine thousand men had occurred in all New England states except Rhode Island.[36] In January 1787 the Shaysites moved from reform to rebellion. On 25 January 1787 approximately fifteen hundred farmers attempted to capture a federal arsenal in Springfield, a key step in their attempt to topple the government of Massachusetts.[37] In that battle four Shaysites were killed and twenty were wounded. After the defeat at the arsenal, the ambit of action was reduced to raids against prominent shopkeepers, military leaders, and lawyers.[38] Powerful legislative and military action against the insurgents finally brought the rebellion to an end in June 1787.[39] The issues raised by Shays' Rebellion were, however, kept alive in the debates over the ratification of the Constitution.[40]

32. Ibid., 38.
33. Ibid., 43.
34. Ibid., 56.
35. Ibid., 58.
36. Ibid., 59.
37. Ibid., 91–102.
38. Ibid., 91.
39. Ibid., 106.
40. Ibid., 120–34.

The desire for frontier independence and resistance to national taxation schemes were additional antecedents of revolutionary direct action. In the late eighteenth century the frontiersmen of western Pennsylvania fiercely resisted the excise taxes on whiskey and other items imposed by the national Congress. Federal agents who tried to collect the tax were frequently assaulted. In the Whiskey Rebellion fifty men marched on the house of tax collector James Neville on 16 July 1794. They demanded that Neville resign and turn over his records concerning the tax on spirits. Neville refused, and on the following day a mob of between four and eight hundred returned and torched Neville's house and barn. One or two men died and several were wounded. By the end of the rebellion seven thousand citizens marched on Pittsburgh and destroyed property. The rebellion spread to Maryland, Virginia, and Kentucky. President Washington mobilized nearly thirteen thousand militia to stop the insurgency. The central demand was a cessation of the tax, but many of the settlers sought independence from the union.[41]

In the summer of 1776 people who lived on the borders of Virginia and Pennsylvania declared independence from those states. The Watauga region of North Carolina also wanted to join the confederacy as an independent state. "It seemed clear to the hopeful founding fathers of the state of Westylvania [part of Pennsylvania]," historian Thomas Slaughter writes, "from the Revolutionary principles ringing loudly in their ears, that 'no country or people can be either flourishing, happy or free . . . whilst annexed to or dependent on any province, whose seat of government is . . . four or five hundred miles distant, and separated by a vast, extensive and almost impassible tract of mountains.' " No state readily accepted the secession of one of its regions. Even when Vermont, then legally a part of New

41. Thomas P. Slaughter, *The Whiskey Rebellion* (New York: Oxford University Press, 1986), 31.

York, requested statehood on 2 July 1777, the Continental Congress denied the petition.[42]

One of the most important characteristics of early American democracy was direct action. This action took the form of petitions, protest demonstrations, and violence. While at first direct action was a means of expressing economic grievances, it became a way for people to take power into their own hands. The next step in attaining truly popular government was to design democratic political institutions.

Democracy Institutionalized   After the United States declared independence from England, the colonies became states, and each state had to find a new basis for governing. The politics of the state constitutions is a highly complex matter. There were many different constitutions in the various states, and not all of them were democratic. Democratic-sounding preambles do not always reflect the true nature of the document. For example, the preamble to the 1780 Massachusetts Constitution seems very democratic in tone, but David Szatmary points out in *Shays' Rebellion*:

> The constitutions of many New England governments further enhanced the position of the commercial elite. . . . The Massachusetts Constitution of 1780 raised provincial property qualifications for officeholding by 50 percent. . . . Samuel Eliot Morison has written: "The Constitution of 1780 . . . was a lawyers' and merchants' constitution, directed toward something like quarter-deck efficiency in government, and the protection of property against democratic pirates."

On the other hand, E. P. Douglass in *Rebels and Democrats* writes:

42. Ibid., 33–34.

It is easy to underestimate the importance of the reforms embodied in even the most conservative of the first state constitutions. If these instruments were far from democratic and if they maintained the framework of traditional institutions, they nevertheless inaugurated the freest governments that the world had seen since ancient times.[43]

In *On Revolution* Hannah Arendt implies that the opponents of the more conservative state constitutions and the national Constitution were an anarchic minority that confused freedom and liberty. She sweepingly praises the state constitutions written and ratified after the American Revolution without sufficiently distinguishing them and their various provisions. By implying that the opponents of the state constitutions were irresponsible enemies of stable government, Arendt ignores the possibility that the dissenters wanted to create enduring institutions, albeit more democratic ones, as much as the colonial elite did.[44]

Political debate in the states often centered upon the drafting and ratification of new state constitutions. Although not uniformly egalitarian, the most democratic of the state constitutions provided for highly representative governments characterized by dominant legislatures with weak executives, frequent rotation in office, minimum property requirements for white male suffrage, and bills of rights. All of these features were found in the most democratic of the state constitutions, that of Pennsylvania in 1776.[45]

The Pennsylvania Constitution had an all-powerful unicameral legislature. There was no governor, but instead a plural

43. Szatmary, *Shays' Rebellion*, 49; Douglass, *Rebels and Democrats*, 68. See also Donald S. Lutz, *Popular Consent and Popular Control: Whig Political Theory in the Early State Constitutions* (Baton Rouge: Louisiana State University Press, 1980), and *The Origins of American Constitutionalism* (Baton Rouge: Louisiana State University Press, 1988).

44. *On Revolution* (New York: Penguin, 1986 [1963]), esp. 141–43.

45. For the text of the Pennsylvania Constitution of 1776, see Morison, *Sources and Documents*, 162–76. See also Foner, *Tom Paine*, 131–32.

executive elected by the people; the executive branch could not
veto the acts of the assembly. Property holding was not a
requirement for state office, and all men over twenty-one who
paid taxes could vote. Debtors not guilty of fraud could not be
imprisoned after losing their property to their creditors. For
fourteen years conservatives and democrats waged a battle over
the Pennsylvania Constitution. Its defenders were the Constitutionalists; in 1790 elitist opponents of the Constitution, called
Republicans, won the battle, putting a new Constitution in
place.[46]

Democrats sought to create through the state constitutions a structure of political power that ordinary citizens could
understand and in which they could easily participate. According to historian Robert Taylor, the call for a "constitution" by
the Berkshire Constitutionalists referred not simply to a written
set of laws or a particular description of state offices but to
"direct popular participation in the choice of offices at all
levels."[47] Only a government that was visible to the people,
whose operations were clearly understood, could be held to
account by ordinary citizens. Democrats rejected the argument
of John Adams and others that in order to attain liberty through
government restraint, political power had to be highly checked
and balanced.[48] The democrats echoed the medieval argument
for undivided authority, which linked the common good with
a united ruling body, rather than the conservative Whig theory
of divided powers.[49] On this point Tom Paine, a powerful
influence on the radicals, agreed with the direct democrats.
"The more simple anything is," he said, "the less disordered

46. Main, *Political Parties Before the Constitution,* 177–78.
47. Robert J. Taylor, *Western Massachusetts in the Revolution* (Providence, R.I.:
Brown University Press, 1954), 83.
48. Merrill Jensen, "Democracy and the American Revolution," *Huntington
Library Quarterly* 20 (August 1957): 331. See also John Adams, "Thoughts on Government," in Hyneman and Lutz, *American Political Writing,* 1:401–9.
49. See Ewart Lewis, "The Contribution of Medieval Thought to the American
Political Tradition," *American Political Science Review* 50 (1956): 462–74.

and the easier repaired when disordered."[50] In the state governments, simplicity meant legislative domination and a one-house
legislature.[51] One radical democrat wrote:

> One branch of Legislature is much preferable to more
> than one, because a plurality causes perpetual contention
> and waste of time. . . . Had the *Romans* been a true
> Democracy, without a Senate, or body different from
> the Plebians, they might have avoided those jars and
> contentions which continually subsisted between those
> two bodies. . . . The simplest mode of legislation is
> certainly the best.[52]

Most of the early state constitutions were written by
legislative councils, but by 1780 radical democrats insisted that
state constitutions be written in conventions elected by the
people and then ratified by popular elections.[53] The Berkshire
Constitutionalists objected to the provisional rule of the Massachusetts government of 1774–75 because it had not been
chosen by the people.

> We chuse to be known to future posterity [read a 1775
> petition from Pittsfield] as being of the Number of those
> who have timely protested against the Reasumption of
> this discordant Constitution, & shall be restless in our
> endeavours that we may obtain the previlege of electing
> our civil & military officers. . . . [W]e pray that every
> town may retain the previlege of nominating their Justice
> of the peace & every County their Judges as well as the
> Soldiers of every Company of the Militia their officers.[54]

50. "Common Sense," in *The Thomas Paine Reader,* ed. Michael Foot and Isaac
Kramnick (New York: Penguin Books, 1987), 68–69.
51. Jackson Turner Main, "Government by the People: The American Revolution and the Democratization of the Legislatures," *William and Mary Quarterly,* 3d ser.,
23 (July 1966): 391–407.
52. "The Interest of America," *American Archives* 6 (June 1976): 842.
53. Lutz, *Popular Consent,* 83.
54. Robert J. Taylor, ed., *Massachusetts, Colony to Commonwealth* (New York:
W. W. Norton, 1961), 19.

When the Massachusetts General Court in the fall of 1776 asked 260 towns whether it was the appropriate body to draft a state constitution, Boston replied:

> To form Government & establish a Constitution for the present & succeeding Generation, is a Task or Consideration the most important, it extends as much to our *Religious* as *Civil Liberties* & includes our *All*—It effects every Individual; every Individual therefore ought to be consulting, acting & assisting. . . . The Means or Channels of Information should lay open to the People, & not restricted or confined to any particular Assembly however respectable.[55]

The radicals wanted the state constitutions to embody democracy. Democracy in this context meant simple government, not one that was checked and balanced, a strong legislature and a weak executive, minimal or no property requirements for white male suffrage, and bills of rights restraining governmental power. Not only did the specific provisions of the constitutions matter to the democrats, but so did the method by which the documents were written and ratified— that is, in constitutional conventions whose representatives were elected by the people—and submitted to the people for their approval. The democrats did not invariably think of their state governments in isolation from the larger country. They wanted to link the state governments in fraternal confederation, but one that would not undermine democracy.

Articles of Confederation   The Articles of Confederation, the first attempt at national government after the Revolution, bound the states in a national structure, yet also guaran-

---

55. Taylor, *Massachusetts, Colony to Commonwealth,* 44. See also Lewis, "The Medieval Contribution," 472–74.

teed sovereignty to the states over their local affairs.[56] Historian Merrill Jensen claimed that "the Articles of Confederation were the constitutional expression of [the] democratic movement and the embodiment in governmental form of the philosophy of the Declaration of Independence."[57] Under the Articles, the national government had no direct relationship with the people. Economic historian E. James Ferguson has written that the provision in the Articles of Confederation forbidding the Congress to tax the people directly expressed a sophisticated understanding of the need for a democratic political economy.

> The power of the purse was . . . the determinant of sovereignty, and upon its location and extent depended the power of government, the existence of civil rights, and the integrity of representative institutions. Their basic premise was that popular control of taxation ensured the rights of citizens. . . . After independence, they tried to safeguard the sovereignty of their new states under the Articles of Confederation by denying Congress the right to tax.[58]

It is an indication of direct democracy's low esteem in the academy that students learn from their American history and government textbooks that the Articles of Confederation were fatally flawed and plunged early American politics and economy into chaos.[59] It is taken for granted that the effort to

56. For the text of the Articles, see Morison, *Sources and Documents*, 178–86.

57. *The Articles of Confederation*, 15. See also Jensen, "Democracy and the American Revolution," 322; E. S. Corwin, "The Progress of Constitutional Theory Between the Declaration of Independence and the Meeting of the Philadelphia Convention," *American Historical Review* 30 (1924–25): 511–36; and J. R. Pole, "Historians and the Problem of Early American Democracy," *American Historical Review* 67 (1961–62): 638.

58. E. James Ferguson, *The Power of the Purse: A History of American Public Finance, 1776–1790* (Chapel Hill: University of North Carolina Press, 1961), xiv–xv.

59. Madison and Hamilton began this tradition, and much of *The Federalist* is devoted to a ferocious critique of the Articles. See also Madison's "Vices of the Political System, 1787" and Letter to George Washington, 16 April 1787, in *The Mind of the Founder: Sources of the Political Thought of James Madison*, ed. Marvin Meyers (Indianapolis: Bobbs-Merrill, 1973), 82–98. For recent evaluations of the Articles, see Lienesch, *New Order*, 63.

replace the Articles was a pragmatic one, based only on practical necessity, and perhaps even the best way to preserve a portion of democracy. Actually, the campaign against the Articles revealed a nationalist ideology that rejected the crucial elements of direct democracy, beginning with autonomy.[60] Hamilton made this clear in *Federalist* no. 23: "[T]here is an absolute necessity for an entire change in the first principles of the system: That if we are in earnest about giving the Union energy and duration, we must abandon the vain project of legislating upon the States in their collective capacities: We must extend the laws of the Federal Government to the individual citizens of America."[61] Hamilton's goals for the United States—power, expansion, and economic development—were different from those of his democratic opponents. Localists sought a national government that would be harmonious with, and even promote, direct democracy. Historians Jensen and Ferguson have shown that an amended Articles of Confederation would have been viable both economically and politically. The real contention concerning the Articles was a dispute over direct democracy.

I have attempted to sketch an outline of early American democracy. Its key elements included direct action in the form of crowds, demonstrations, and riots; movements for independence from larger states; sustained political and economic campaigns such as the Regulator movement and the Shays and the Whiskey rebellions; attempts to create or preserve democratic state constitutions written by popular conventions and ratified by the people; and the preservation of the Articles of Confederation, which guaranteed states autonomy over their own

60. Merrill Jensen, "The Idea of a National Government During the American Revolution," in *Essays on the Making of the Constitution*, ed. Leonard Levy (New York: Oxford University Press, 1969), 61–87. My contention is not that the democrats wanted to preserve the Articles without change, but that they, as opposed to the nationalists, saw the Articles with some amendments as a fit framework for the nation whereas the nationalists wanted to discard the Articles altogether. See Lienesch, *New Order*, 80.

61. No. 23 in *The Federalist*, ed. Jacob E. Cooke (Middletown, Conn.: Wesleyan University Press, 1961), 148.

affairs. In order to more fully comprehend the nature of early American democracy, one must understand its origin. Why did the democratic moment occur?

II

Actually, there were several antecedents of early American political culture: (1) the colonial charters; (2) the New England Puritan tradition of town meetings and covenanted communities; (3) the throwing off of deference by the lower classes, largely the result of the dissemination of Whig political theory, which radicals interpreted literally, emphasizing its most democratic elements; and (4) a desire on the part of small farmers to maintain a traditional communitarian way of life.[62]

Charters   The seeds of self-government were planted in most of the northern colonies at the time of their founding.[63]

62. Scholars disagree on the issue of when the decentralization of power in early America commenced. They acknowledge that by the end of the seventeenth century an oligarchy had taken power in each colony, but they disagree on whether the democratization movement began in the 1690s or after the American Revolution. Those who say it began earlier stress the importance of community as the basis of democratic localism in the eighteenth century. See Michael Zuckerman, *Peaceable Kingdoms* (New York: Knopf, 1970); Gary B. Nash, *The Urban Crucible* (Cambridge: Harvard University Press, 1979); and Bruce C. Daniels, *Town and Country: Essays on the Structure of Local Government in the American Colonies* (Middletown, Conn.: Wesleyan University Press, 1978), 7. Others emphasize the American Revolution as the catalyst for decentralist movements. See John M. Murrin, "Review Essay," *History and Theory* 11 (1972): 270; Charles Andrews, *Colonial Self-Government, 1652–1689* (New York: Harper and Bros., 1904), 68; and Main, *Political Parties Before the Constitution*, 15–16. It is not crucial for my argument to decide which factor was most important in producing early American democracy or when precisely that democratic moment began. It is enough here to note both the communitarian and revolutionary antecedents of early democratic radicalism.

63. Lutz, *Origins*, chap. 4. See also Lutz, ed., *Documents of Political Foundation Written by Colonial Americans* (Philadelphia: Institute for the Study of Human Issues, 1986).

The charters of Rhode Island, Massachusetts, and Connecticut "embodied levelling doctrines of the rank and file of the Army in the days of the second Civil War. . . . [They] encouraged and gave legal warrant to democratic government in America."[64] The charters and other founding documents were at once governmental constitutions and expressions of political principles.[65] When the King of England revoked the charter of Massachusetts in 1689, the Puritans revolted to regain self-governance, mounting a battle for autonomy nearly one hundred years before the American Revolution. In Gary Nash's account, the turning point for early American decentralization of power was the Puritan overthrow of the English-appointed Governor of Massachusetts, Edmund Andros, in 1689. The rebellion, Nash says, led the people of the colony to desire more power.

> It was this feeling of political importance, and the dawning notion that the public good was better served if the common people exercised a watchdog role rather than electing eminent men to positions of power and trusting them to exercise it for the commonweal, that marked a turning point in politics.[66]

The Puritan Legacy   The first generation of Puritans might well have deprecated their democratic progeny as a licentious mob. After the initial schemes of town and church government laid the groundwork for both authority and democracy, the Puritan leaders and ordinary citizens entered a protracted struggle for power. Thus, the Puritans left the United States two legacies. One was centralist, national, and hierarchical. The

64. Andrews, *Colonial Self-Government*, 68–69.
65. Andrews called the 1681 Concessions and Agreements of West New Jersey "the best that the political thinkers of the time could furnish . . . a true constitution" (ibid., 121).
66. *The Urban Crucible*, 41–42.

impulse towards centralization took the form of increased powers for both the General Court and church synods, at least until 1691.[67]

Nevertheless, as detailed in the last chapter, the Puritans also left a localist inheritance. Although Puritan practice became more centralized, Congregationalist ideas had filtered into secular thinking and promoted democracy. According to historian Edmund Morgan, "That republican ideas . . . should be congenial in the colonies, was due in the first place to the strong Calvinist tradition which had been nourished over the years by the American clergy."[68] The ideal of small, covenanted, participatory community spread throughout the colonies alongside of Lockean individualism.

Whig Theory   Whig theory, derived from John Locke, the Scottish enlightenment, and the English Commonwealthmen, emphasized individual and collective rights against arbitrary power.[69] The Declaration of Independence remains the most succinct American statement of Whig theory, insisting as it does on the right of each people to "dissolve the political

67. Perry Miller, *The New England Mind: From Colony to Province* (Boston: Beacon Press, 1953). The nationalist impulse of the Puritans has been emphasized by Sacvan Bercovitch in *The American Jeremiad* (Madison: University of Wisconsin Press, 1978). See also Zuckerman, *Peaceable Kingdoms*, 15.

68. "The American Revolution as an Intellectual Movement," *Paths of American Thought*, ed. A. Schlesinger, Jr., and M. White (Boston: Houghton Mifflin, 1963), 11–33. See also Alice M. Baldwin, *New England Clergy and the American Revolution* (Durham, N.C.: Duke University Press, 1928), and Claude Van Tyne, "Influence of the Clergy, and of Religious and Sectarian Forces, on the American Revolution," *American Historical Review* 19 (October 1913): 44–64.

69. On the political theory of the American Revolution, see Bernard Bailyn, *The Ideological Origins of the American Revolution* (Cambridge: Harvard University Press, 1973), and Caroline Robbins, *The Eighteenth-Century Commonwealthmen: Studies in the Transmission, Development and Circumstance of English Liberal Thought from the Restoration of Charles II until the War with the Thirteen Colonies* (Cambridge: Harvard University Press, 1959). See also Gordon S. Wood, *The Creation of the American Republic, 1776–1787* (Chapel Hill: University of North Carolina Press, 1969); Lienesch, *New Order*; Schaar, ". . . And the Pursuit of Happiness," in *Legitimacy,* 231–50; and Garry Wills, *Inventing America: Jefferson's Declaration of Independence* (New York: Vintage, 1978).

bands which have connected them with one another, and to assume among the powers of the earth . . . separate and equal station."[70] After stating the principle of autonomy for collectivities, Jefferson declares the existence of natural rights that no government can violate. If a government does transgress those rights, then "it is the right of the people to alter or to abolish it" and to create new governments. Thus, three great Whig principles evoked in the Declaration are autonomy of collectivities, natural rights (not explicitly mentioning the right so cherished by conservative Whigs, the right to private property), and the legitimacy of revolution.

In order to gain their support for and participation in the American Revolution, colonial leaders taught Whig theory to the rank and file and stirred them to revolt.[71] The radicals learned their Whig theory through newspapers, sermons, and popular pamphlets such as Paine's *Common Sense* and the anonymous pamphlet, "The People the Best Governors."[72] The Revolution provided a political education for the small farmers.[73] After the Revolution, the people refused to become deferential again. They applied the lessons of the American Revolution to politics at home. Thomas Allen, one of the Berkshire Constitutionalists, said, "If the right of nominating to office is not invested in the people we are indifferent who assumes it whether any particular persons on this side or the other side of the [w]ater."[74] Invoking similar sentiments, Shays' Rebellion was conducted in the vocabulary of the American Revolution. In the eyes of the elite, the common people were so many Calibans who said: "You taught me language, and my profit on't / Is, I know how to curse."[75]

70. "Declaration of Independence," in *The Portable Thomas Jefferson*, ed. Merrill D. Peterson (New York: Viking, 1975), 235.

71. Maier, *From Resistance to Revolution*, 48, 86, 88, 94.

72. Ibid., xiv., 27–35. "The People the Best Governors" can be found in Hyneman and Lutz, *American Political Writing*, 1:390–400.

73. Taylor, *Western Massachusetts*, 175–76; Szatmary, *Shays' Rebellion*, 64.

74. In Taylor, *Massachusetts, Colony to Commonwealth*, 19.

75. *The Tempest*, act 1, sc. 2, lines 363–64.

The elite themselves recognized that Whig leaders had helped to create the radical democratic movement. After the outbreak of the New York Tenant Rebellion of 1766, General Thomas Gage said that the Whig leaders

> certainly deserve any losses that they sustain for it is the work of their own hands. They first sowed the seeds of Sedition amongst the People and taught them to rise in Opposition to the Laws. What now happens is a consequence that might be easily foreseen after the Tumults about the Stamp Act.[76]

The same sentiment was echoed later by Fisher Ames, who said that the Shays' insurgents had "turned against their teachers the doctrines, which were inculcated in order to effect the late revolution."[77] Henry Knox, Secretary of War for the Confederation during the American Revolution, grasped the radical nature of the ideology of Shays' Rebellion and the extension of Whig political teachings into the economic realm. In a letter to the Marquis de Lafayette, Knox implies that the people have improperly applied Whig political principles to economics, confusing popular sovereignty in elections with a right to shape the economy and to invoke majority rule to threaten the right of private property:

> Opinions which perhaps were excessively disseminated previous to and during the revolution, seem to produce effects materially different from what were intended. For instance, the maxim that all power is derived from the people, and that all is influenced by a certain proportion of the people . . . to mean an annihilation of debts, and a division of property . . . [The following is crossed out in Knox's letter.] and that the government of the people,

76. In Douglass, *Rebels and Democrats*, 59.
77. In Szatmary, *Shays' Rebellion*, 98.

means that the people shall participate of the property of the wealthy by a mode different and less fruitful than industry. The object and ultimate end of republican government thus delusively established in their minds they have no hesitation of embracing any means for the accomplishment of their purposes.[78]

I have suggested, and the testimony of the radicals and elite leaders has confirmed, that the Whig theory upon which the American Revolution was based reinforced ideas of self-government and participation that were inherited by ordinary colonists. But I have also argued throughout this essay that liberal theory is, in important respects, antithetical to genuinely popular government. Key elements in Whig theory tended to undermine direct democracy. These included the right to private property even when that right conflicted with equality and the common good[79]; representation as an unproblematic substitute for direct participation in power; the replacement of actual affirmation of a covenant with tacit consent; the rejection of the past and tradition, an emphasis on abstract reason in the place of customary and experiential knowledge, and the idea that in the state of nature all individuals were fundamentally separate so that community and politics are taken to be unnatural. These

78. Knox to Marquis de Lafayette, 13 February 1787, Henry Knox Papers, Massachusetts Historical Society, Boston.

79. Democratic radicals modified the Whig idea of property, but they did not abandon it. See Foner, *Tom Paine,* 39–41. The radicals perpetuated the Puritan belief that individuals should "use their property consistently with the ethical sense of the community and with the preservation of the community's economic and social stability" (William E. Nelson, *The Americanization of the Common Law* [Cambridge: Harvard University Press, 1975], 6). Also see Zuckerman, *Peaceable Kingdoms,* 70, 77. The radically democratic amendments of the Whig theory of property are significantly different from its mainstream liberal rendering. For example, in *Federalist* no. 10, James Madison was unwilling to place any restrictions on property ownership even though he conceded that a society based on private property would be highly divided and would find it difficult to attain an objective standpoint from which to adjudicate competing claims of interest. Whereas Madison had asserted that the protection of private property was the chief aim of the new national government, the anonymous author of the radically democratic pamphlet "Interest of America" said only, "We must come as near a new form of Government as we can, without destroying private property" (35).

aspects of Whig theory tend to erode direct democracy's base in community, political participation, a concern for the common good, equality, and parochial knowledge. But if Whig ideas are synonymous with liberalism, how could they provide the fuel for a radically democratic movement?

The answer to this question is twofold, having to do with Whig theory's content and the radicals' mode of interpreting that theory. It must be admitted that, along with its undemocratic tenets, Whig theory contained democratic elements.[80] These included the foundation of government in the compact of the people, the right of citizens to choose their leaders and to hold them accountable for their actions, equality of political power, the right to overthrow unjust government, and the principle that each political entity should rule itself.[81] The Whig idea of collective self-rule was a lesson widely learned in the American Revolution. That the Revolution was a war for local control is a point so obvious that it is often forgotten. To be ruled by an outside power was taken to be a symbol of either infancy or tyranny; a politically mature country was independent from every other country. Radical democrats applied this lesson within the United States. If state governments did not respect the rights of the people, each community retained the legitimate power to revolt against that government and create a new one.

When early American radical democrats interpreted Whig theory, they stressed its most democratic elements, but they also read the theory in a literal way that brought out its most revolutionary implications. Conversely, in order to undermine the radical implications of Whig theory, the Federalists

---

80. See Sheldon S. Wolin, "What Revolutionary Action Means Today," *democracy* 2:4 (Fall 1982): 17–28, reprinted in John Rajchman and Cornel West, eds., *Post-Analytic Philosophy* (New York: Columbia University Press, 1985).

81. In summarizing the principle of autonomy during this period, Edmund Morgan wrote: "The people of one region ought not to exercise dominion over those of another, even though the two may be joined together. . . . Every people is entitled, by the law of nature and of nature's God, to a separate and equal station" ("The American Revolution as a Social Movement," 27).

and other liberal theorists construed its terms figuratively.[82] Perhaps the most radical move of the democrats was to take literally the Whig doctrine of popular sovereignty. In a statement that has been called "an extension to the right of revolution hitherto unheard of outside of the pages of Rousseau," Benjamin Hichborn defined civil liberty as

> not a 'government by laws', made agreeable to charters, bills of rights or compacts, but a power existing in the people at large, at any time, for any cause, or for no cause, but their own soveren pleasure, to alter or annihilate both the mode and essence of any former government, and adopt a new one in its stead.[83]

This literal application of the doctrine of popular sovereignty could be used to challenge undemocratic colonial institutions, as it was in Thomas Allen's declaration:

> We have always been persuaded that the people are the fountain of power. . . . [T]he first step to be taken by a people . . . for the Enjoyment or Restoration of Civil Government amongst them is the formation of a fundamental Constitution. . . . We have heard much of the Government being founded in Compact. What compact has been formed as the foundation of Government in this province?[84]

82. In *Popular Consent and Popular Control*, political theorist Donald S. Lutz describes the process somewhat differently. He writes, "The theory evolving from the colonial political experience made it natural to appropriate English Whig political ideas, and then to bend these ideas to meet American needs. . . . [The Federalists] ultimately rejected many Whig political symbols to create the political theory still dominant in the United States" (xv). Whereas Lutz asserts that the Federalists rejected Whig symbols, I would say that the Federalists preserved the symbols, but interpreted them figuratively. In chapter 5 I will explore a concrete instance of this type of de-radicalizing Federalist construction, namely, their rendering of the popular sovereignty doctrine. See also Maier, *From Resistance to Revolution*, 46.

83. Corwin, "The Progress of Constitutional Theory," 517–18; Benjamin Hichborn, "Boston Oration: March 5, 1777," in *Principles and Acts of the Revolution in America*, ed. Hezekiah Niles (Baltimore: William Ogden Niles, 1822), 47.

84. Taylor, *Massachusetts, Colony to Commonwealth*, 28.

Even today citizens might ask themselves: What say have we had in creating the political and economic institutions under which we live? Who has asked for our consent? When have our own institutions been legitimated by the explicit consent of the people?

Early American democracy had several sources, including the Puritan legacies of covenanted community and autonomy, the loss of deference during the American Revolution, and the widespread dissemination of Whig political theory that the radicals interpreted literally and selectively. One final source of early American democracy remains to be discussed: the political economy of eighteenth-century America.

III

One classic interpretation of early American political economy has steered political theorists away from the democratic radicals to whom historians have paid far more attention. The great theorist Louis Hartz asserted that citizens of the United States were uniformly middle-class at the time of the nation's founding and were, therefore, liberals in their political theory. There was no proletariat or aristocracy to serve as the basis of a genuinely radical or conservative theoretical tradition.[85] By "radical" I mean not violent or uncontrolled political action, but the possession of highly divergent values and a fundamentally different outlook on the world. Hartz did not celebrate America's lack of an indigenous radicalism, as some have suggested, but he may not have established the best criteria for the existence of a radical tradition. Genuine class differences for

85. *The Liberal Tradition in America* (New York: Harcourt, Brace, and World, 1955); and "American Political Thought and the American Revolution," *American Political Science Review* 46 (June 1952): 321–42.

Hartz seem to have required divisions as deep as those of feudal Europe; genuinely radical theory for Hartz had to be as profoundly divergent from mainstream thought as those of Rousseau and Marx. In applying the criteria that he did, Hartz may have missed the unique radicalism of early America. Hartz's powerful thesis, that most American political thought has been fundamentally liberal, was so generally correct that it has led theorists to ignore instances of American politics that escaped the liberal room, wholly or in part.

Recent historical research has revealed that significant social differences did exist among early Americans. Thus, following Hartz's logic, it is reasonable to assume that the various groups within the society had different worldviews.[86] Historian E. P. Thompson wrote that a class exists "when some men, as a result of common experiences (inherited or shared), feel and articulate the identity of their interests as between themselves, and as against other men whose interests are different from (and usually opposed to) theirs." And, according to Thompson, class consciousness is "the way in which these experiences are handled in cultural terms: embodied in traditions, value-systems, ideas, and institutional forms."[87] Employing Thompson's definitions, there were significant differences of class and class consciousness in early America.

Early American political culture was divided between democratic communitarians, most of whom were small farmers or urban artisans, and elite Whigs, who were either merchants or owners of large farms. Each group possessed its own vision of the public good: the small farmers and artisans wished to preserve traditional, small-scale communitarian institutions; the merchants and large landowners desired commercial growth and expansion, to be accomplished with the aid of an increas-

86. For evidence that deep economic divisions existed in early America, see references above to Jensen, Taylor, and Ferguson. For an opposing view, see Robert E. Brown, *Middle Class Democracy and the Revolution in Massachusetts* (Ithaca, N.Y.: Cornell University Press, 1955).

87. *The Making of the English Working Class* (New York: Vintage, 1963), 9–10.

ingly powerful and centralized national government. Although, of course, some of the artisans and small farmers adopted the worldview of the elite, and some members of the upper classes worked to preserve small communities, it was primarily artisans and yeoman farmers who provided the chief momentum in the movement to preserve local autonomy, while the upper classes constituted the driving force for a strong national government.[88]

The contrasting political visions of the wealthy and the poor in early America were revealed during the economic crises of the mid-eighteenth century. The farmers in Massachusetts and most of the other colonies depended upon merchants for cash and supplies because the farmers' property was largely in land and livestock. During the planting season the farmers borrowed heavily from the merchants. When the merchants themselves faced cash shortages as they did during the depression of 1740, after the American Revolution, and during the inflation of 1780, they foreclosed on their loans to the farmers.[89]

The farmers, having little cash, offered to repay their debts by other means including barter, specie, and certificates.[90] The merchants usually rejected these substitutes, which led to a marked increase in attendance at debtor courts and in jail populations. Regularly faced with the prospect of foreclosure and prison, the farmers sought relief from their state governments, which, they had been told, were supposed to enact their will and serve their interests. At the state level they challenged the undemocratic nature of land-grant control, speculation, and forms of currency. They requested from the state governments

88. See Szatmary, *Shays' Rebellion*; Slaughter, *Whiskey Rebellion*, 14, 104, 133.

89. This historical account is derived from Jensen, "Democracy"; Taylor, *Western Massachusetts*; Main, *Political Parties Before the Constitution*; E. James Ferguson, "Political Economy, Public Liberty, and the Formation of the Constitution," *William and Mary Quarterly*, 3d ser., 40 (July 1983): 389–412; John C. Miller, "Religion, Finance, and Democracy in Massachusetts," *New England Quarterly* 6 (March 1933): 29–58; and Szatmary, "New England Merchants and the Chain of Debt," in *Shays' Rebellion*, 19–36.

90. See "Petition of a County Convention," in Morison, *Sources and Documents*, 210–14.

the issuance of paper money and tender laws that would permit barter to be substituted for cash. In addition, they called for a shift of governmental aid from the merchants to the farmers.

Before the Revolution a central economic proposal of the small farmers was the creation of land banks, which would issue currency based on "the security of real property."[91] Some colonial assemblies procured Parliament's aid in squashing these land-bank proposals.[92] The collaboration of their assemblies with Parliament and with the wealthy elite revealed to the farmers that control of their political institutions "rested, not in the hands of the majorities of voters, but in the hands of a very small group of men," and they set out to change those institutions.[93] Thus, the struggles of the farmers to cope with their financial difficulties developed into a political and economic program that sought to recast colonial institutions into a more democratic mold. Although at first democrats in Massachusetts, North Carolina, and other colonies "only sought some form of paying their debts compatible with an agricultural society," they eventually advocated more extensive political and economic reforms.[94]

Hartz dismissed the Shays rebels as "small capitalist[s] in the American backwoods" who chiefly feared losing their own private property.[95] That may have been their fundamental worry, but it is wrong to equate concern for their small farms with narrow-minded individualism. For the Shaysites, property implied independence and a traditional democratic and communitarian way of life.[96] Szatmary writes of Shays' Rebellion:

> Undeniably, the rebellion became primarily a contest between two economic classes: yeomen who faced the

91. Ferguson, "Political Economy."
92. Ferguson, The Power of the Purse, 5–7.
93. Jensen, The Articles of Confederation, xv–xvi.
94. Szatmary, Shays' Rebellion, 43.
95. Hartz, The Liberal Tradition, 73–74.
96. Petition from the Town of Greenwich, Mass., 16 January 1786, in Morison, Sources and Documents, 208–10; Szatmary, Shays' Rebellion, esp. chaps. 1 and 2.

loss of their properties, and merchants, lawyers and speculators who stood to gain from these losses. But without neglecting the economic basis of the turmoil, it seems clear that Shays' Rebellion can be more fully understood as an economic conflict exacerbated by a cultural clash between a commercial society and a rural, subsistence-oriented way of life.[97]

The effort to protect a traditional way of life remains an essential part of democratic radicalism. It is large-scale capitalism and the centralized state that seeks not only to take power from the people but to regularly transform the way ordinary people work and live. To resist that transformation is one constituent of democracy.[98]

Early American democracy should inspire democrats today. In our own time radical transformation, at least in the United States, often seems impossible. Our political and economic institutions are already in place, and the fundamentals cannot be altered without making matters worse. There is little room for creativity, and no money in the budget to pay for it. If ways could be found to ameliorate crime, drugs, pollution, unemployment, and poverty without raising taxes, that would be vision enough. Only a handful of people seem to care about politics today. In contrast, to look at America during the period of the Revolution is to discover in our own past a political culture in which people were not so passive, when they were forcefully and directly involved in public life.[99]

97. Szatmary, *Shays' Rebellion*, 18.
98. See Sheldon S. Wolin, "Archaism, Modern, and *Democracy in America*," in *The Presence of the Past* (Baltimore: Johns Hopkins University Press, 1989), esp. 77–81.
99. Of course, sadly, even radical democracy in this period did not generally include women, American Indians, or African–Americans. It may be some compensation for past wrongs if women, Indians, and African-Americans find inspiration from earlier radicals for their struggles to extend the parameters of democracy in America today.

IV

Democracy in early America appeared in several guises: crowds and direct action, participatory state constitutions written in popularly elected conventions and ratified by the people, highly autonomous communities that did not overwhelm average people or exclude them from political participation, and the creation of a political economy that would be compatible with those communities. The localists had a set of values fundamentally different from those of the wealthy liberal leaders of the United States. The localists wanted to protect a tradition of participation and community from the onslaught of a powerful, and ultimately triumphant, movement that sought to centralize government and restore order through the curtailing of political participation.

The radically democratic culture of early America had a number of different sources: Puritan traditions of covenanted, participatory, autonomous communities; a desire on the part of ordinary people to preserve those communities against encroachment by a commercial elite; and the loss of deference toward authority accompanied by a liberal interpretation of Whig ideas broadly disseminated during the American Revolution.

Democratic localist politics in early America was not primarily ideological; it was expressed more in action than in words. The localists lived their ideas: they constituted a political culture and sought to create political and economic institutions compatible with that culture. They lacked, however, a fully articulated political theory, one that would reveal the connection between democracy and community and between democracy and the conservation of the early American political tradition. The fashioning of such a theory was the task of the Antifederalists.

4

The Antifederalists and the Conservative Dimension of Democracy

ike Hegel's Owl of Minerva, the Antifederalist owl flew at dusk. On the eve of the long decline of American localism, the Antifederalists produced its most articulate theoretical expression. The Antifederalists attempted to clarify the nature of democracy in order to preserve it. They resisted the Federalist revolution because it threatened a form of political life that was precious to them. The Antifederalists believed that the American state-republics were the freest polities in the world since those of ancient Greece. Although the states were not uniformly democratic, they were highly egalitarian and participatory when compared to most governments in the world at that time. Democratic customs, practices, and sentiments had developed among the citizens of the various states that the Antifederalists wanted to protect from the encroachment of the national government.

The Antifederalists were conservatives who defended democracy. The fact that these terms are usually taken to be antithetical in the American political vocabulary may help to explain why the Antifederalists have been described in such contradictory and pejorative terms by their most eminent interpreters. Because they have not employed the appropriate vocabulary to understand it, scholars have frequently denigrated Antifederalist thought as muddled liberalism.[1] Because the greatest American political thinkers, such as Madison, Paine, and Jefferson, the last commonly mistaken for an Antifederalist, have written in the liberal tradition, the Antifederalists have appeared second-rate in comparison.[2] But when seen in the combined light of the conservative and democratic theoretical traditions, Antifederalist thought constitutes an important con-

1. Gordon S. Wood describes the Antifederalists in highly pejorative terms in "Interestedness and Disinterestedness in the Making of the Constitution," in *Beyond Confederation: Origins of the Constitution and American National Identity,* ed. Richard Beeman, et al. (Chapel Hill: University of North Carolina Press, 1967), 69–109, and in *The Creation of the American Republic, 1776–1787* (New York: W. W. Norton, 1969), 483–536. Cecilia Kenyon portrays the Antifederalists as paranoid liberals in her introduction to *The Antifederalists* (Indianapolis: Bobbs-Merrill, 1966) and in "Men of Little Faith: The Antifederalists on the Nature of Representative Government," in *The Reinterpretation of the American Revolution: 1763–1789,* ed. Jack P. Greene (New York: Harper and Row, 1968), 526–66. Herbert J. Storing's interpretation of Antifederalist thought is more subtle than that of Wood or Kenyon, but he too declares that the Antifederalists were, ultimately, confused liberals. See his essay *What the Anti-Federalists Were For,* vol. I of *The Complete Anti-Federalist,* 7 vols., ed. Herbert J. Storing (Chicago: University of Chicago Press, 1981). Jackson Turner Main, *The Antifederalists* (Chapel Hill: University of North Carolina Press, 1961), and Robert A. Rutland, *The Ordeal of the Constitution: The Antifederalists and the Ratification Struggle of 1787–1788* (Boston: Northeastern University Press, 1983 [1966]), call the Antifederalists "democrats," but do not distinguish democracy from liberalism. My view of the Antifederalists as conservative democrats is close to that of Wilson Carey McWilliams, "Democracy and the Citizen: Community, Dignity, and the Crisis of Contemporary Politics in America," in *How Democratic Is the Constitution?,* ed. Robert A. Goldwin and William A. Schambra (Washington, D.C.: American Enterprise Institute, 1980), 79–101, and of Michael Lienesch, "In Defense of the Antifederalists," *History of Political Thought* 4:1 (February 1983): 65–87. James H. Hutson has summarized the history of scholarship on the Antifederalists in "Country, Court, and Constitution: Antifederalism and the Historians," *William and Mary Quarterly,* 3d ser., 38 (July 1981): 337–68.

2. On Jefferson's relationship with the Antifederalists, see Rutland, *Ordeal,* 89–90, 216–17.

tribution to American political theory: it offers an alternative to the liberalism of the Federalists and of Paine and Jefferson.

I

The difficulty in ascertaining the political identity of the Antifederalists can, in part, be attributed to the fact that they spoke in many voices and were eclectic in their borrowings from various theoretical schools. And although they often addressed common themes, they did not jointly and systematically develop a political theory, as did the authors of *The Federalist*. I have arrived at my own interpretation of Antifederalism by emphasizing certain passages over others. I am particularly interested in those aspects of Antifederalist political thought that do not echo Jefferson or the Federalists. I have tried to delineate the distinctive contribution that the Antifederalists made to the American political tradition, emphasizing what is unique in their thought at the risk of distorting its actual proportions.

Perhaps my most provocative claim is that the theories of democracy and conservatism share many important elements. To those who are familiar with the critique of liberalism formulated by radical democratic communitarians, the proposition may appear less surprising. Sheldon Wolin, John Schaar, Wilson Carey McWilliams, and Michael Rogin have all strongly criticized liberalism for its individualism that undermines political community.[3] Schaar has posited authority, which liberalism

3. See Sheldon S. Wolin, *Politics and Vision* (Boston: Little, Brown, 1960), 293–94 and passim, "The New Conservatives," *New York Review of Books* 23:1 (6 February 1976), 6–11, and "The People's Two Bodies," *democracy* 1:1 (January 1981): 9–16; John H. Schaar, *Legitimacy in the Modern State* (New Brunswick, N.J.: Transaction Press, 1981), esp. 53–55, 193–209; Wilson Carey McWilliams, "Politics," *American Quarterly* 35 (1983): 19–38, esp. 27, and "Reinhold Niebuhr: New Orthodoxy for Old Liberalism," *American Political Science Review* 56 (1962): 874–85; and Michael Paul Rogin, *Ronald Reagan: The Movie* (Berkeley: University of California Press, 1987), 134–41 and passim.

deprecates, as an essential component of community. Wolin, Schaar, and McWilliams have stressed the importance of tradition and memory in the preservation of community. The values put forward by these radical communitarians are in part derived from the Athenian polis. They are also taken, although profoundly altered, from the conservative philosophy of Edmund Burke. The contemporary radicals found material in Burke to develop a radical theoretical alternative to liberalism.[4] I suggest here only that the Antifederalists combined democracy and conservatism in a similar way first.

In order to discern the similarities between conservative and democratic theory, one might begin by recognizing their common antagonism to liberalism. Liberalism values individual rights and a strong state to protect these rights. Liberalism rejects authority and tradition; it creates a society of high mobility and incessant change. Enlightenment liberalism posits the existence of natural laws (hidden from experience, but discernible by reason) and the ability of enlightened leaders to apply these laws to society and human beings until both are perfected.[5]

In contrast, conservatism can be understood as a defense of traditional society against the revolutionary liberal politics of the Enlightenment. Conservatives respect tradition. Burke particularly valued tacit knowledge based on sentiment and participation in customs. The Enlightenment, represented in America by Paine, Franklin, Jefferson, and the Federalists, has been too directly linked with democracy, and its opponents with elit-

---

4. It must be admitted that the matter is somewhat complicated because there are Lockean elements in Burke's political thought. Democratic radicals, needless to say, do not emphasize those elements.

5. See Peter Gay, *The Enlightenment: An Interpretation,* 2 vols. (New York: Alfred A. Knopf, 1967), and Henry Steele Commager, *The Empire of Reason: How Europe Imagined and America Realized the Enlightenment* (Garden City, N.Y.: Doubleday/ Anchor, 1977). On the Enlightenment's opposition to parochial knowledge, see Thomas J. Schlereth, *The Cosmopolitan Ideal in Enlightenment Thought: Its Form and Function in the Ideas of Franklin, Hume, and Voltaire, 1694–1790* (Notre Dame: University of Notre Dame Press, 1977).

ism.[6] While the liberal revolution paved the way for "mass democracy" with its highly expanded suffrage, guarantees of free public speech, and the elimination of property restrictions on holding political office, it has at the same time undermined the conditions necessary for direct democracy: small, stable community; decentralized government; and respect for custom, local knowledge, and parochial loyalty. These elements of traditional society are valued by both conservatives and radical democrats.

Enlightenment liberalism undermines both conservatism and radical democracy. Liberal political culture has proven to be barren ground for the development of a genuinely conservative political theory. Liberal society, wrote Sheldon Wolin, is "so passionately dedicated to change that the only consistent conservatives may be the conservationists."

> A traditionless society that conserves nothing; ruling groups that are committed to continuous innovation; social norms that stigmatize those who fail to move away: such a society presents a formidable challenge to the conservative imagination.

Liberal society, Wolin argues, has "erased most peculiarities of place, of settled personal and family identity, and made men and women live by an abstract time that is unrelated to personal experience or local customs."[7] The abilities to live in abstract time and to be preoccupied with issues distant from one's own

6. See, for example, Commager, *Empire of Reason,* 36–37. For the elitism inherent in the liberal enlightenment, see Schaar, "Some Ways of Thinking About Equality," in *Legitimacy,* 167–70.

7. "The New Conservatives," 6–8. Marx made a similar point in the *Communist Manifesto* (New York: International Publishers, 1948) when he wrote (12): "Constant revolutionizing of production, uninterrupted disturbance of all social conditions, everlasting uncertainty and agitation distinguish the bourgeois epoch from all earlier ones. All fixed-frozen relations, with their train of ancient and venerable prejudices and opinions, are swept away, all new-formed ones become antiquated before they can ossify."

experience are usually developed only by a small number of "experts" or specially trained individuals.[8] If the possessions of such abilities are demanded as the condition for being entrusted with power, then government will be restricted to the few.

The affinity that exists between direct democracy and conservatism is revealed by the writings of the Antifederalists who were both democratic and conservative. As democrats, the Antifederalists believed in highly autonomous political communities and in the participation of the common people in such political arenas as town meetings, grand juries, political clubs, constitutional conventions, and direct action. The conservative dimension of the Antifederalists can be seen in the theoretical subjects with which they were concerned: custom and experience, scale and distance, and the tension between diversity and uniformity. Whereas modern democratic theory emphasizes individual rights, Antifederalist thought focused on communities. The Antifederalists believed that each community has an identity expressed in its customs and that a truly democratic government reflects and protects the identity of the locality.

Community, custom, tradition, experiential knowledge, and local loyalties, terms that constitute the Antifederalist vocabulary, are ideas derived not from liberal thought, but from the conservative theoretical tradition. These themes are central in the works of two authors generally considered to be the most important conservative theorists of the eighteenth century: David Hume and Edmund Burke. The Antifederalists selectively employed a conservative vocabulary similar to that of Hume and Burke to develop a democratic political theory. In pointing out the similarities between Antifederalist arguments and the ideas of Burke and Hume, I do not mean to suggest that the latter were democrats or the sources for the theory of the former, although it is interesting to note that in Storing's

8. The term "expert" is defined in Alfred Schutz, "The Well-Informed Citizen: An Essay on the Social Distribution of Knowledge," in Arvid Broderson, ed., *Studies in Social Theory*, vol. 2 of *The Collected Papers of Alfred Schutz* (The Hague: Martinus Nijhoff, 1964), 120–34.

collection of Antifederalist writings Hume is mentioned four times and each time approvingly.[9] I recognize that great differences existed not only between the theories of the English and Scottish conservatives and those of the Antifederalists but also between Hume and Burke. The Antifederalists wanted to preserve a far more democratic society than did Burke, and they had little praise for authority. The Antifederalists were not skeptics and had far more sympathy than did conservative elitists for human limitations; what Hume at times derided as sentiment and parochialism, the Antifederalists accepted and respected.

The only reason to compare the theories of the Antifederalists with those of Burke and Hume is to see the extent and nature of Antifederalist conservatism. Despite the differences among their positions, the Antifederalists, Burke, and Hume shared certain understandings concerning human nature and the political importance of sentiment and custom. Like Hume and Burke, the Antifederalists placed at the center of their theory local custom, regional character, and the diverse identities of communities.[10] And all three described human beings as essentially parochial. They thought, as did the Federalists, that people tend to care most about themselves and those who are close to them; their loyalty extends only to those governments that they feel a part of and that reflect their customs. Most people, they said, possess tacit knowledge, the sources of which

9. *The Complete Anti-Federalist,* 2.6.43, 3.5.10, 4.3.28, 6.14.146. On the relationship of Hume and American political thought, see John M. Werner, "David Hume and America," *Journal of Historical Inquiry* 33:3 (July–September 1972): 439–56; Melvin H. Buxbaum, "Hume, Franklin, and America: A Matter of Loyalties," *Enlightenment Essays* 3:2 (Summer 1972): 93–105; and Douglass G. Adair, "That Politics May Be Reduced to a Science: David Hume, James Madison, and the Tenth *Federalist,*" in *The Reinterpretation of the American Revolution,* 487–503. Of course, Edmund Burke's greatest work and the one with the most affinities to Antifederalist thought, *Reflections on the Revolution in France,* was written in 1790, after the struggle over the ratification of the Constitution. Thus, my argument is not that Antifederalist political thought is derived from Hume and Burke, but that it has surprising affinities with the theories of those authors.

10. See especially Hume, "Of National Characters," in *Essays: Moral, Political, and Literary,* ed. Eugene F. Miller (Indianapolis: Liberty Classics, 1985), 197–215.

are experience, local custom, and sentiment, rather than abstract reason; and in most people the passions rule reason. On this matter, the Antifederalists would have sided with Burke, not Paine. The Antifederalists and Burke distrusted innovation, even though they wanted to protect different kinds of societies from change: the Antifederalists wanted to preserve a democracy; and Burke, a constitutional monarchy and traditional social distinctions. Whatever their similarities with conservative elitists, the Antifederalists were political alchemists: they took arguments and ideas that Burke and Hume used to defend a traditional, hierarchical society and transformed them into democratic political thought.

The connection between conservatism and democracy can be seen with special clarity in the struggle between the Federalists and Antifederalists over the ratification of the Constitution. In that battle the Antifederalists wanted to preserve the old order and resist change while the Federalists were the radical innovators.[11] Herbert Storing wrote:

> One of the most striking and, to many readers, surprising aspects of the debate over the Constitution is the conservative posture of the opposition. The Anti-Federalists did not deny the need for some change, but they were on the whole defenders of the status quo. They deplored departures of the Constitution from "the good old way" of "the antient and established usage of the commonwealth."[12]

Storing correctly calls the Antifederalists conservatives, but does not fully recognize the radically democratic nature of the society that the Antifederalists wanted to conserve. The Anti-

    11. See Michael Lienesch, *New Order of the Ages: Time, the Constitution, and the Making of Modern American Political Thought* (Princeton: Princeton University Press, 1988), 141–45.
    12. *What the Anti-Federalists Were For,* 7. See also "The Maryland Farmer," in *The Complete Anti-Federalist,* 5.1.21.

federalists were not fighting to protect an abstract principle such as federalism, but to preserve the political culture that had developed in early America before the passage of the Constitution.

The Federalists openly acknowledged that they were innovators who wanted to overcome and overturn the democratic political culture of early America.[13] In writing to George Washington before the Constitutional Convention, James Madison called for "radical attempts" to change the old order.[14] He insisted in *The Federalist* that the Constitution sought to reverse the direction of early American politics: "The novelty of the undertaking immediately strikes us. . . . [T]he existing confederation is founded on principles which are fallacious. . . . [W]e must consequently change this first foundation, and with it, the superstructure resting upon it."[15] The principles to which Madison referred were those of localism and direct democracy, principles that the Antifederalists sought to conserve under an amended Articles of Confederation.[16] Hamilton also claimed to have discovered a radical new form of political science to replace the democratic tradition. He wrote:

> The science of politics . . . like most other sciences, has received great improvement. The efficacy of various principles is now well understood, which were either not known at all, or imperfectly known to the ancients.[17]

13. See Michael Lienesch, "Interpreting Experience: History, Philosophy, and Science in the American Constitutional Debates," *American Politics Quarterly* 11:4 (October 1983): 384–86.

14. April 16, 1787, *The Papers of James Madison*, vol. 9, ed. Robert Rutland and William M. E. Rachal (Chicago: University of Chicago Press, 1975), 383.

15. No. 37 in *The Federalist*, ed. Jacob E. Cooke (Middletown, Conn.: Wesleyan University Press, 1961), 233. See also Lienesch, "Interpreting Experience," 391.

16. Lienesch, *New Order*, 122–23.

17. *Federalist* no. 9, 50–51. See also Wood, *Creation*, 593–615, and J. G. A. Pocock, *The Machiavellian Moment* (Princeton: Princeton University Press, 1975), 506–52.

The Antifederalists rejected the Federalists' new political science.[18] "The Maryland Farmer" wrote, "There is nothing solid or useful that is new— . . . if every *political institution* is not fully explained by Aristotle, and other ancient writers, yet there is no *new* discovery in this most important of all sciences for ten centuries back."[19] Like Burke, the Antifederalists felt a "sullen resistance to innovation."[20] "We know," wrote Burke,

> that *we* have made no new discoveries; and we think that no new discoveries are to be made, in morality; nor in the great principles of government, nor in the ideas of liberty, which were understood long before we were born.[21]

In the eyes of the Antifederalists, the new Federalist political science was elitist innovation, having as its aim the decrease of direct political participation and the substitution for it of the rule of enlightened representatives.[22] The Antifederalists found more support for direct popular rule in the tradition of political theory than in the Federalists' new political science.[23]

I have argued that the Antifederalists were conservative democrats, and in part their conservatism resulted from their desire to preserve the democratic political culture in early America. The Antifederalist stance toward early American political culture is not particularly relevant to the situation of democrats today. To conserve political institutions today would

18. On the different uses of history by the Antifederalists and Federalists, see Lienesch, *New Order,* chap. 5.

19. *The Complete Anti-Federalist,* 5.1.21. See also Wood, *Creation,* 600–651, and Lienesch, *New Order,* 126–31.

20. *Two Classics of the French Revolution: Edmund Burke, "Reflections on the Revolution in France," Thomas Paine, "The Rights of Man"* (New York: Doubleday, 1989), 99.

21. Ibid.

22. On elitist elements of Federalist theory, see Kirk Thompson, "Constitutional Theory and Political Action," *Journal of Politics* 31:3 (August 1969): 655–81.

23. "The Maryland Farmer," in *The Complete Anti-Federalist,* 5.1.21. The civic humanist tradition in political theory is described by J. G. A. Pocock in *The Machiavellian Moment.*

be to preserve the Federalist principle of centralization, not Antifederalist localism. Yet other elements of Antifederalist conservative democratic theory should not be ignored in any modern revival of democracy: these include a respect for local custom, a desire to link custom and power, and a respect for experiential knowledge and local loyalty.

II

The Antifederalists delighted in variety and feared uniformity. They valued the preservation of local identities as much as they did freedom of speech or protection of property. According to the Antifederalists, each state was a unique polity that possessed a different set of manners and customs that constituted its particular identity. The "customs" that expressed and established the local identity might be defined as the habitual practices of a people who have lived together over time in a particular place. One function of government, the Antifederalists believed, was to complement and preserve this identity. When government conflicted with these customs, either the local identity would be undermined or the government would fall because it would lose the allegiance of the people.

The conviction that the national government would violate the local customs of the various states and destroy the democratic character of early Americans was the essence of the Antifederalist critique of the Constitution. The guarantee of state sovereignty contained in the Articles of Confederation permitted local governments to make laws appropriate to the character and customs of their communities, whereas the Constitution, they thought, would create uniform rule that would eventually obliterate local customs and character. They subscribed to Montesquieu's assertion that "more states have perished because their *moeurs* have been violated than because their laws have been broken."[24]

"The Federal Farmer" wrote: "Different laws, customs, and opinions exist in the different states which by a uniform system of laws would be unreasonably invaded."[25] Similarly, "Agrippa" stated:

> The inhabitants of warmer climates are dissolute in their manners, and less industrious, than in colder countries. A degree of severity is, therefore, necessary with one which would cramp the spirit of the other. . . . To promote the happiness of the people it is necessary that there be local laws. . . . It is impossible for one code of laws to suit Georgia and Massachusetts. They must, therefore, legislate for themselves.[26]

The framers of the Constitution, wrote another Antifederalist, desired "with massive curbs, to break us . . . into a uniform, sober pace, and thus, gradually, tame the *troublesome* mettle of the freeman."[27] The very size of the national government and the tremendous area it ruled would overawe the average person, leaving him feeling helpless to understand or to affect his own government.[28] "The same government pervading a vast extent of territory," wrote "The Maryland Farmer," "terrifies the minds of individuals into meanness and submission."[29]

The Antifederalists could have found philosophical sanc-

24. In *The Political Theory of Montesquieu*, ed. Melvin Richter (New York: Cambridge University Press, 1977), 157.

25. *The Complete Anti-Federalist*, 2.8.14. Storing thus summarized the Antifederalist position: "A national government would be compelled to impose a crude uniform rule on American diversity, which would in fact result in hardship and inequity for many parts of the country" (*What the Anti-Federalists Were For*, 15–16). Of course, the Antifederalists would have also opposed a variety of rules for different localities based only upon executive discretion.

26. *The Complete Anti-Federalist*, 4.6.16.

27. "Cato Utincensis," in ibid., 5.7.6.

28. Kenyon, *The Antifederalists*, 214, 209.

29. *The Complete Anti-Federalist*, 5.1.53.

tion in the writings of David Hume for their argument that a
national government issuing uniform laws would undermine or
alter local customs and character. Hume believed both in the
existence of regional characters and in the ability of political
institutions and leaders to affect those characters. Although
Hume thought that human behavior is to a large degree the
same in all places and times, he wrote, "there are also characters
peculiar to different nations and particular persons, as well as
common to mankind."[30] "Each nation has a particular set of
manners . . . ," he suggested in his essay "Of National Characters."[31] Hume argued that government, leaders, history, economic condition, relations among nations, and race are the
primary determinants of local identity.[32] Of these, the most
important are government and leaders. An oppressive government, Hume said, changes the temper of a people, and political
leaders who place the public good ahead of private interest can
elevate the popular character.[33] The Antifederalists most feared
a scenario described by Hume: "A very extensive government
. . . established for many centuries . . . spreads a national
character over the whole empire, and communicates to every
part a similarity of manners."[34]

The division between the Antifederalists and the Federalists concerning the value of local diversity and the right
relationship between political power and community identities
is replicated in many contemporary political debates. Many
people respect, even cherish, distinctive American regions and
religious and ethnic neighborhoods. America, they assert with
pride, is a nation of nations, a patchwork quilt, a land of
immigrants. Most of what is best in American culture emerged
from a particular community. Many regret that communities
have been destroyed because freeways were put through them,

30. *A Treatise on Human Nature*, ed. L. A. Selby-Bigge (New York: Oxford
University Press, 1978), 403.

31. *Essays: Moral, Political, and Literary*, 197.

32. Ibid., 204–7.

33. Ibid., 203.

34. Ibid., 204.

or because the buildings became too old and run down, or because the children all moved away. Much of American literature and film laments the destruction of local communities.[35]

But Americans are often simultaneously inclined to see the dangers of diversity rather than its riches. The preservation of local identity conflicts with the ideal of integration. Local identities, it is said, tend to produce chauvinism and conflict.[36] And the question must be faced: What degree of divergence from the democratic principles of equality, respect for particular groups within the larger community, and freedom of speech can a democratic country permit in one of its polities? The problem can be seen in the Antifederalist defense of local self-rule that was cited above: "The inhabitants of warmer climates are dissolute in their manners, and less industrious, than in colder countries. A degree of severity is, therefore, necessary with one which would cramp the spirit of the other. . . . They must, therefore, legislate for themselves."[37] "Agrippa" implies that Southern governments cannot allow the degree of active citizen participation with which New Englanders can be trusted, and that democratic autonomy is compatible with severe laws.

Southerners themselves later adopted a version of this argument, seeking to protect local customs from encroachment by the national government.[38] To this day the South has a predilection for severity. Whereas most large cities have abandoned corporal punishment in the schools, it is still practiced in

35. See William Adams, "Natural Virtue: Symbol and Imagination in the American Farm Crisis," The Georgia Review 30:4 (Winter 1985): 695–712, and Richard Lingeman, Small Town America (Boston: Houghton Mifflin, 1980), esp. 441–81.

36. Yet see Schaar, "The Case for Patriotism," in Legitimacy, 285–311, and Mary Parker Follett, The New State: Group Organization the Solution of Popular Government (Gloucester, Mass.: Peter Smith, 1965 [1918]).

37. The Complete Anti-Federalist, 4.6.16.

38. Anne Norton describes the Southerners' position: "The South, it was argued, had developed—indeed had always possessed—a culture and character distinct from the remainder of the nation. A confederacy, limited in its jurisdiction and powers, might answer the requirements of sections diverse in interest and character. A national, consolidated government could not." Alternative Americas (Chicago: University of Chicago Press, 1986), 111.

the South and in other rural areas.[39] "We feel our policy [on corporal punishment] fits the community in which we live," said a school superintendent in Georgia.[40] A *New York Times* reporter wrote, "particularly in the more rural, conservative reaches of the South and Midwest, the practice of corporal punishment is so rooted in local customs and culture that it is sanctioned by state law."[41]

How much local severity can be tolerated in a democracy? What if cultural differences are invoked to justify police brutality or violence against women and children or racial or ethnic minorities? Clearly, such brutality is unacceptable; it should not be ignored or condoned by other communities. It must be noted, however, that the liberal language of individualism, privacy, and private property has also been effectively used to justify violence: "He's my kid, and I have a right to hit him if I want to; what I do in my house is no one's business but my own." With regard to community autonomy, intervention in the affairs of other communities may not require depriving the community of its essential sovereignty. Interposition could take the form of moral suasion, public outcry, or economic sanctions rather than the creation of a supreme national or international authority that would be expected to act everywhere to apply universally defined justice. This is, of course, not a radical stance, or even a relativistic one, but a description of present practice in regard to moral outrages committed in other countries.

Ironically, the dream that some great power could comprehend justice and distribute it everywhere with a mighty hand has helped to legitimate the greatest potential threat to justice and democracy. Increasingly, citizens turn to the least democratic branch of a national government for aid in fighting local power in the name of civil rights and civil liberties. As worthy as these goals are, it must be recognized that each victory

39. *New York Times*, 14 January 1987, sec. 12, p. 1.
40. Ibid.
41. *New York Times*, 9 July 1987, p. 22A.

increases the legitimacy, and therefore the power, of the national government; and because they have relied on legal remedies to their problems, the people's habits and capacity for political action continue to atrophy.[42]

Whereas many people today equate democracy with individual rights, Antifederalist democratic thought centered on communities. The Antifederalists believed in natural rights, but did not conceive of these as individual rights against all collectivities, but instead as the right of communities not to be oppressed by state or national governments, and the right of minorities not to be oppressed by majorities.[43] The Antifederalists did not reduce democracy to voting for representatives and written guarantees of individual rights. Their democratic thinking was based on a conception of the individual that antedated liberalism. Whereas liberalism conceived of individuals as politically isolated beings endowed separately with inalienable rights, the Antifederalists respected and sought to preserve a conception of human beings as individuals-in-communities that was articulated in the conservative tradition.

III

Enlightenment liberalism put forward two descriptions of human intellectual and political capacities, neither of which were appropriate for direct democracy. One, found in Tom Paine, was an idealized portrait of men and women as bearers of universal reason. Paine argued as if each citizen were a Socrates. All people, as part of their common sense, had the capacity to receive universal truths. He wrote:

42. As a community organizer, I regularly heard from the members that hiring a lawyer to solve a particular problem would be preferable to taking action.
43. Kenyon, *The Antifederalists,* 154, 167. See also McWilliams, "Democracy and the Citizen," 92.

[G]overnment in a well constituted republic, requires no belief from man beyond what his reason can give. He sees the *rationale* of the whole system, its origin and its operation; and as it is best supported when best understood, the human faculties act with boldness, and acquire, under this form of government, a gigantic manliness. . . . As to the prejudice which men have from education and habit, in favor of any particular form or system of government, those prejudices have yet to stand the test of reason and reflection. In fact, such prejudices are nothing.[44]

Paine's "appreciation" of the common people not only damned them with false praise but devalued the actual sources of their wisdom: sentiment, experience, authority, tradition, and custom. By setting up universal reason as the proper standard of political knowledge, Enlightenment liberalism cleared the path for elitist arguments that said, in effect, because the people do not, for whatever reasons, possess abstract reason they are not fit to directly wield political power.

The Federalists thought the ability to reason abstractly was a qualification for political rule that the people did not, generally, possess; the Federalists deprecated customary, experiential, and local knowledge, and they portrayed human beings as ambitious, rapacious, and selfish. The Federalists identified parochialism with self-interest and justified the removal of the average person from political power by arguing that such a separation was required to attain justice and the common good. Contending that the people were unqualified to directly rule themselves, the Federalists designed a government that would temper, refine, check, and balance the popular will. Denying any correspondence between local knowledge and the intelligence required to govern a large nation, Madison sought to

44. *Two Classics of the French Revolution,* 379, 393. For Burke's defense of prejudice, see 100–120.

create a political system led by "representatives whose enlightened views and virtuous sentiments render them superior to
local prejudice."[45] Because confederacies were based on parochial knowledge, the Federalists saw them as hopelessly flawed
forms of national government.[46] At the national level, said
Madison, leaders had to possess a "knowledge of national
circumstances and reasons of state. . . . A strong predilection in
favor of local objects . . . can hardly fail to mislead the
decision."[47] In a striking and profoundly antidemocratic image,
Alexander Hamilton expressed his fear that being too close to
the people might infect their representatives. He said, "Can a
democratic assembly, who annually revolve in the mass of the
people, be supposed to pursue the public good?"[48]

The Antifederalists rejected that whole way of thinking.
The Antifederalists had no contempt for the human desire to
live in a world of familiar people and things, nor for the average
person's inattentiveness toward or failure to understand distant
political matters. The Antifederalists believed that most people
care only about things that they directly experience; affections
do not reach to distant objects. In politics, the people cherish
and respect only that government and those leaders who reflect
their local culture and of whom they have a personal knowledge.

Rather than removing the people from power because of
their parochial nature, the Antifederalists sought to limit power
to the human scale.[49] They rejected the "fashionable language"
that "the common people have no business to trouble them-

45. Wood, *Creation*, 505.
46. See *The Papers of Alexander Hamilton*, vol. 3, ed. H. C. Syrett and Jacob E.
Cooke (New York: Columbia University Press, 1962), 1:655, 3:82; and Max Farrand,
ed., *The Records of the Federal Convention of 1787*, rev. ed., 4 vols. (New Haven: Yale
University Press, 1937), 1:378.
47. *Federalist* no. 15, 97. See also Wood, *Creation*, 494–501; Wood, *Beyond
Confederation*, 73; and *The Mind of the Founder*, ed. Marvin Meyers (Indianapolis: Bobbs-
Merrill, 1973), 56.
48. Farrand, *Records*, 1:299.
49. See Kirkpatrick Sale, *Human Scale* (New York: Coward, McCann, and
Geoghegan, 1980).

selves about government."[50] In their call to preserve popular rule, the Antifederalists saw the need to restrict the size and complexity of the national government. Only a government so limited could be understood by ordinary citizens. "Cato" warned that "from the vast extent of your territory, and the complication of interests, the science of government will become intricate and perplexed, and too mysterious for you to understand."[51] A government that left most political power in the localities and that was designed to make its operations apparent could be controlled by citizens who possessed limited, but not negligible, political wisdom. While many Antifederalists criticized the Constitution for insufficiently dividing power, the Antifederalist "Centinel" endorsed the Pennsylvania Constitution of 1776 as a model of a people's government. He wrote:

> A republican, or free government, can only exist where the body of the people are virtuous, and where property is pretty equally divided. In such a government the people are the sovereign and their sense or opinion is the criterion of every public measure. . . . The highest responsibility is to be attained in a simple structure of government, for the great body of people never steadily attend to the operations of government, and from want of due information are likely to be imposed on—If you complicate the plan by various orders, the people will be perplexed and divided in their sentiments about the sources of abuses and misconduct, some will impute it to the senate, others to the house of representatives, and so on, that the interposition of the people may be rendered imperfect or perhaps wholly abortive.[52]

50. *The Complete Anti-Federalist*, 3.3.3.
51. Ibid., 2.6.14. "Agrippa" calls for checks and balances in Kenyon, *The Antifederalists*, 153.
52. Kenyon, *The Antifederalists*, 7.

What is most attractive in this passage is "Centinel's" sympathy with the political psychology of ordinary people. The Antifederalists believed that institutions had to be preserved or designed that would be appropriate for people's nature, and that would not render irrelevant their tacit knowledge.

The Antifederalists valued the knowledge possessed by the people, knowledge constituted by custom, experience, sentiment or passion, and familiarity with local circumstance. Like Burke, the Antifederalists believed in "the moral constitution of the heart."[53] "Government is a science," said the Antifederalist "Alfred" of Philadelphia, "which consists more in experience than in notional knowledge. What will suit the different manners, habits, and interests of a wide extended country like America, can only be known by an *experiment*."[54] Experience would teach the people how to recognize and to choose the policies that would best suit them. To place experience, rather than an abstract science, at the heart of political knowledge is to say that ordinary people have access to politically relevant wisdom without having to make extraordinary efforts to attain it.

To suggest that the Antifederalists respected experiential or tacit knowledge is not to imply that they denigrated the importance of political theory. But they thought that political theory was incomplete without local knowledge; political success required both.[55] After all, the great political actors and thinkers had been unable to solve the perennial problems of politics despite the fact that "from Moses to Montesquieu the greatest geniuses have been employed on this difficult subject."[56] The policies of large empires always failed, wrote "Agrippa," because the laws were not "made by the people who felt the circumstances."[57] The knowledge of circumstance, an essential

53. *Two Classics of the French Revolution*, 94.
54. *The Complete Anti-Federalist*, 3.10.7.
55. *The Documentary History of the Ratification of the Constitution*, vol. 1, ed. Merrill Jensen (Madison: State Historical Society of Wisconsin, 1976), 215.
56. *The Complete Anti-Federalist*, 5.6.1.
57. Kenyon, *The Antifederalists*, 133.

component of legislative wisdom, was tacitly possessed by the people. The Antifederalists believed that the proper design of political institutions encouraged civic participation by the many. Although the people are parochial, and often self-interested, the Antifederalists thought that well-designed political institutions that encouraged popular participation would induce citizens to care for the common good. "The Maryland Farmer" wrote: "Our people are capable of being made any thing, that human nature was or is capable of, if only we have a little patience and give them *good* and wholesome institutions."[58] In short, the Antifederalists believed that the tacit knowledge possessed by average citizens qualified them for direct self-rule, but only in a certain context: that of decentralized institutions that encouraged political participation.

The Antifederalists were democrats who shared with their elitist opponents a view of human nature as being local and parochial. But unlike elitist conservatives and liberals, the Antifederalists believed that human nature could be improved, if not perfected. By designing participatory institutions, human beings could be led to care for the common good. And whereas the Federalists took their interpretation of human nature to be grounds for removing people from power, the Antifederalists believed that government should be shaped to human scale.

IV

Few in the eighteenth century appear to have disputed the fact that most human beings are parochial: on that point the Antifederalists, Federalists, Hume, and Burke agreed. Hume wrote that affections do not extend much beyond the localities:

58. *The Complete Anti-Federalist*, 5.1.52.

Contiguous objects must have an influence much superior to distant and remote. Accordingly, we find in
common life, that men are principally concerned about
those objects, which are not much removed either in
time or space, enjoying the present, and leaving what is
far off to the care of change and fortune.[59]

Edmund Burke believed that the locality was the beginning of
our public affection, but not the end:

To be attached to the subdivision, to love the little
platoon we belong to in society, is the first principle (the
germ as it were) of public affections. It is the first link in
the series by which we proceed towards a love to our
country and mankind.[60]

The Antifederalists derived from this eighteenth-century view
of human nature a democratic argument against the possibility
of large-scale popular government. The Antifederalist "Cato"
disputed the possibility of being loyal to a distant government.
He wrote that the principles that bind families and citizens are
"in their exercise, like a pebble cast on the calm surface of a
river, the circles begin in the center, and are small, active, and
forcible, but as they depart from that point, they lose their
force, and vanish into calmness."[61] The localist theory of human nature implied that the people would withhold their allegiance from a national government in a large country because
it would be out of the range of their senses.

As a result, the Antifederalists believed, and Hamilton
feared, the national government would either fall or would have
to maintain its power through coercion. "The general government," asserted the "Federal Farmer," "far removed from the

59. *A Treatise on Human Nature*, 428. See also 306, 318, 320, 324, 352, and 534.
60. *Two Classics of the French Revolution*, 59.
61. *The Complete Anti-Federalist*, 2.6.19.

people . . . will be forgot or neglected, and its laws in many cases disregarded, unless a multitude of officers be continually kept in view, and employed to enforce the execution of the law."[62] Hamilton did not dispute this statement because he shared Antifederalist and conservative assumptions about the limited range of human loyalties; he too believed that the large scale of the new nation posed severe problems for making it seem legitimate in the eyes of the people. The Antifederalist solution was to maintain the sovereignty of the states under the Articles of Confederation. The Federalists developed the doctrine of popular sovereignty.

Until the Federalists' political and theoretical victory, the concepts of community, participation, custom, experiential knowledge, local loyalty, and the common good were central to the American political vocabulary. Before the Federalists could attain passage of the Constitution, they had to convince the nation that these were the wrong terms for thinking about politics. The Federalists denigrated local custom and tacit knowledge as an inadequate foundation for empire and claimed that direct democracy was inevitably excessive and threatening to liberty, especially to the right of private property. They said that communities that were guaranteed autonomy would inevitably war with each other. In changing America's political values, the Federalists thus accomplished a revolution in theory as great as the one they engineered in American politics. Nevertheless, the transition from Antifederalist to Federalist conceptions of politics was not easily achieved; it required convincing Americans that their democratic ideals would be preserved in the new institutions created by the Constitution.

62. Kenyon, *The Antifederalists*, 214.

5

The Ghostly Body Politic: The Federalist Papers and Popular Sovereignty

espite the explicitly antidemocratic statements of the Federalists, Americans persist in describing the government they designed as a democracy. I contend that the confusion in the American mind about the relationship of their political system to the democratic ideal was deliberately created by the Federalists. In order to clarify this matter, I would like to describe the relationship between popular sovereignty and democracy in the political thought of the Federalists Alexander Hamilton and James Madison. It is necessary to understand Federalist political theory accurately in order to comprehend the true nature of American politics today. The Federalist identification of popular sovereignty with popular government continues to dominate contemporary thinking about democracy; actually, it is the

Federalist doctrine of popular sovereignty that is embodied in our political institutions.[1]

My argument is based on the following assertions: (1) Alexander Hamilton and James Madison, whom I will refer to as the Federalists, often spoke as if they were democrats even though they opposed direct democracy. (2) Although their rhetoric sounded democratic, in fact the Federalists employed the vocabulary of popular sovereignty. Democracy and popular sovereignty are significantly different: (a) popular sovereignty is consistent with strong central government but democracy is not; (b) popular sovereignty, unlike direct democracy, does not require the ongoing and active political participation of the people; (c) because popular sovereignty has been confused with democracy, its political implications have not been fully explored—popular sovereignty and direct democracy are based on two different conceptions of political power: democracy, which tries to limit governmental power so that ordinary people can understand and wield it, and popular sovereignty, which creates enormous power for the central government. (3) The Federalists reformulated the doctrine of popular sovereignty and thus shaped a new direct relationship between the national government and the people because they feared that the people might not support the powerful central government created by the Constitution. The revised doctrine and the new relationship were intended to gain popular backing for the government and to undermine the formation of a public that could direct the operation of that government. In short, the Federalists' great accomplishment in political theory was to establish an unmediated relationship between the national government and the people that, ironically, discourages democracy.

The pseudodemocratic rhetoric of the Federalists is best

---

1. A typical statement is that of the eminent historian Edmund S. Morgan: "In sum, the American Revolution marked the culmination, in America at least, of a transformation that took government out of the hands of the monarchs claiming to rule by the grace of God and placed it in the hands of the people." "The Problem of Popular Sovereignty," in *Aspects of American Liberty*, ed. G. W. Corner (Philadelphia: Memoirs of the American Philosophical Association, 1977), 112.

understood when seen in the historical context of the genuinely democratic political culture of eighteenth-century America. This was the political order that the Antifederalists sought to protect. The Federalists did not accept this order; they sought to centralize power, to curb participation, and to preserve inequalities of wealth that Madison predicted would develop when the new government more rigorously defended the rights of private property.

Rhetorically, the Federalists conceded to the Antifederalists that all government, including the one defined in the new Constitution, should derive its power from the people, but the Federalists insisted that "the people" meant "we, the people of the United States," rather than the citizens of towns, counties, and states. The chief dispute between the Federalists and the Antifederalists did not concern the best means to empower the people most consistent with protection of individual rights. Rather, the dispute was about ends: the Antifederalists sought to amend the Articles of Confederation in order to better preserve localist democracies; the Federalists sought to replace those democratic cultures with a powerful national government.

I

Given the attention that scholars have recently devoted to the intentions of the Constitutional framers regarding democracy, it may seem surprising that a definitive characterization of those intentions has yet to be established.[2] This confusion is, I submit, understandable because it was deliberately cultivated by the authors of The Federalist. Although in some places the Federal-

2. See, for example, Robert A. Goldwin and William A. Schambra, eds., *How Democratic Is the Constitution?* (Washington, D.C.: American Enterprise Institute, 1980), and Martin Diamond, "Democracy and *The Federalist*: A Reconsideration of the Framers' Intent," *American Political Science Review* 53 (March 1959): 52–68.

ists speak as if they hated democracy, one must admit that they often seem to advocate the creation of a government that would refine and extend the reach of popular will in a large government.[3] At times they even sound like radical democrats.

According to Hamilton, "The fabric of American Empire ought to rest on the solid basis of THE CONSENT OF THE PEOPLE. The streams of national power ought to flow immediately from that pure original fountain of all legitimate authority."[4] Madison says something similar when he defines a republic, such as the government created by the Constitution, as a type of rule "which derives all its power directly or indirectly from the great body of the people."[5] Madison said, "I believe in the name of the people."[6] According to the Federalists, not only does all power emanate from the people, but the people can collectively alter the government at will.[7] Consent, power from the people, the right of revolution—is this not the vocabulary of democracy?

And yet the Federalists made it plain that they rejected "pure" democracy, if "pure" democracy can be defined as equality, participation, and community.[8] In *Federalist* no. 10, Madison said that government's task is not to create equality, but to protect the diverse human faculties that produce inequality.[9] In popular action Madison saw "the danger of oppres-

---

3. See Joseph M. Bessette, "Deliberative Democracy," in *How Democratic Is the Constitution?*, 102–16.

4. No. 22 in *The Federalist*, ed. Jacob E. Cooke (Middletown: Wesleyan University Press, 1961), 146. See also *Federalist* no. 23, 148; no. 28, 178–79; no. 39, 253; no. 49, 340; no. 63, 424–25; and no. 78.

5. *Federalist* no. 39, 251.

6. James Madison, *The Papers of James Madison*, ed. Robert A. Rutland and Charles F. Hobson, vol. 11 (Charlottesville: University Press of Virginia, 1977), 124.

7. See, for example, *Federalist* no. 28, 178.

8. See *Federalist* no. 10, 61–64; Gordon S. Wood, "Democracy and the Constitution," 1–17, and Walter Berns, "Does the Constitution Secure These Rights?," 59–78, in *How Democratic Is the Constitution?*; Cecilia Kenyon, "Alexander Hamilton: Rousseau of the Right," *Political Science Quarterly* 73 (June 1958): 162–68, 175; James Ceaser, *Presidential Selection* (Princeton: Princeton University Press, 1979), 35–49.

9. *Federalist* no. 10, 58.

sion."[10] One glory of the American government, according to Madison, was "the total exclusion of the people in their collective capacity."[11] As for local autonomy and small community, the Federalists opposed these on the very grounds that they encouraged a high degree of political participation.[12] To prevent direct democracy, Madison sought to extend the sphere of government: "Divide et impera, the reprobated axiom of Tyranny, is under certain qualifications, the only policy by which a republic can be administered under just principles."[13] Hamilton's disdain for democracy is perhaps more familiar than Madison's. At the Constitutional Convention, Hamilton declared that the people are incapable of self-rule because they are "too turbulent and changing; a permanent body must be created to check their impulses."[14] On his deathbed, Hamilton called democracy "the real disease" of the nation, a disease that would spread if power were ever decentralized in America.[15]

On the face of it, the Federalists appear to be contradicting themselves. In some places, they seem to heartily support popular power; at other points, far more numerous, they seem to be designing a government in which representation, checks and balances, protection of private property, and expanded national boundaries will all serve to check the aims of the people and to prevent democracy.[16] How can these seemingly opposed sets of Federalist statements be reconciled? Did the Federalists

10. Madison, *Papers* 11:298; Gordon S. Wood, *The Creation of the American Republic, 1776–1787* (New York: W. W. Norton, 1969), 410.

11. *Federalist* no. 63, 428.

12. *Federalist* nos. 14, 15, 17, and 49.

13. Madison, *Papers* 1:214, 9:346, 456; *Federalist* nos. 10 and 51; Robert A. Dahl and Ed Tufte, *Size and Democracy* (Stanford: Stanford University Press, 1973), 10.

14. Max Farrand, ed., *The Records of the Federal Convention of 1787*, rev. ed., 4 vols. (New Haven: Yale University Press, 1937), 1:299. Hamilton also "acknowledged himself not to think favorably of Republican Government" (ibid., 1:424).

15. Gerald Stourzh, *Alexander Hamilton and the Idea of Republican Government* (Stanford: Stanford University Press, 1970), 40.

16. Ceaser, *Presidential Selection*, 53–54, 59; Joseph M. Bessette and Jeffrey Tulis, "Introduction," in *The Presidency in the Constitutional Order* (Baton Rouge: Louisiana State University Press, 1981); and Bessette, "Deliberative Democracy."

know of some way by which the power that emanates from the people could be used to frustrate democracy?

An answer to these questions might appear if they are posed a little differently. If the Federalists were interested in building a strong central government, significantly insulated from popular will, how could they draw power for that government from the people? Why would they even seek to base the power for the central government on the people? Would it not be sufficient to empower the national government by ratifying a Constitution that would give the government broad and expansive powers in its commerce clause, supremacy clause, necessary and proper clause, and in the creation of a national military?[17] The Federalists replied, "No." They did not see the mere ratification of the Constitution as a sufficient source of power for the national government; they believed that these written funds of power would be inadequate and incomplete if the people did not support the government created by the Constitution. The Federalists were forced to embrace the doctrine of popular sovereignty to gain the support of the people, but by embracing it, they hoped to provide the new government with an essential source of power.

This is not to say that either Hamilton or Madison invented the popular sovereignty doctrine. A glance at the history of the idea reveals that the Federalists restored the centralizing potentialities of the doctrine after it had been appropriated, to much different effect, by eighteenth-century American democrats.

II

Popular sovereignty may be understood as an answer to two questions: Where does legitimate political power come from?

17. John W. Burgess, "The American Commonwealth," *Political Science Quarterly* 1 (March 1886): 22; Willmoore Kendall, "On the Preservation of Democracy for America," *Southern Review* 4 (Summer 1939): 53–68.

Where is that power located? In the medieval form of the doctrine, the answer to the first question was "the people"; the answer to the second was often the central government.[18] Those who first formulated the doctrine did not fix the form of the government that possessed the right to speak in the name of the people. The government might be a monarchy or a republic, so long as a central location for power was designated.[19] Advocates of popular sovereignty rejected the idea that power should be derived from God or shared by the monarch and the church; instead, they posited that political power comes from the people. But that did not necessarily imply democracy. As Gierke pointed out, "It was easy to erect a system of Absolute Monarchy upon the original Sovereignty of the People."[20]

During the seventeenth and eighteenth centuries, three groups of political theorists formulated variations of the popular sovereignty doctrine: absolutists, liberals, and radicals. Hobbes, an absolutist, said that government originated as an act of popular will, but once the people had conferred "sovereignty" upon "one man or upon one assembly of men," they gave up their power.[21] John Locke modified Hobbes's account of the transfer of power. Developing the idea of popular consent, Locke made the transmittal of power from the people to their representatives a continuous series of acts rather than a onetime occurrence.[22] Although Locke's version of popular

18. Bernard Crick, *International Encyclopedia of the Social Sciences*, s.v. "Sovereignty." See also A. D. Lindsay, *The Modern Democratic State* (New York: Oxford University Press, 1972 [1943]), 213–29; Walter Ullmann, *A History of Political Thought: The Middle Ages*, especially the chapter "The Sovereignty of the People" (New York: Penguin Books, 1965), 200–229; Michael Wilks, *The Problem of Sovereignty in the Later Middle Ages* (Cambridge, England: Cambridge University Press, 1963), viii; Edmund S. Morgan, *Inventing the People: The Rise of Popular Sovereignty in England and America* (New York: W. W. Norton, 1988).

19. Otto von Gierke, *Political Theories of the Middle Ages*, trans. F. W. Maitland (Boston: Beacon Press, 1958 [1900]), 38.

20. Ibid., 43.

21. Michael Oakeshott, ed., *Leviathan* (Oxford: Basil Blackwell, 1957), 113; Stourzh, *Hamilton*, 48–49.

22. See Sheldon S. Wolin, "The Idea of the State in America," *Humanities in Society* 3 (Spring 1980): 155 and passim; Donald Lutz, *Popular Consent and Popular Control: Whig Political Theory in the Early State Constitutions* (Baton Rouge: Louisiana State University Press, 1980), 39 and passim; and Wood, *Creation*, 346, 371.

sovereignty was more palatable than that of Hobbes to many eighteenth-century Americans, both Hobbes and Locke described a social contract by which people agreed to authorize a government to act in their names rather than to exercise power themselves.

Radicals, both English Whigs and American democrats, reinterpreted the popular sovereignty doctrine. They inferred that if the people are the source of power in society, then they have the right to form governments and to overthrow them whenever they choose to do so and that the people should continue to engage in political action even when their representatives are meeting. Whereas Hobbes and Locke had said that the people must transfer their power to representatives, radical Whigs asserted that the people always retain political power.[23] The radical democrats believed that popular sovereignty denoted the regular participation by all citizens in every aspect of government: elections, instruction of representatives, juries, constitutional conventions, town meetings, and direct action.[24] Although not always a democrat, Benjamin Hichborn epitomized the radical democratic position when he declared that he would not accept elections or written guarantees of rights as sufficient makers of popular power. "Civil liberty," he said, in a statement cited in chapter 3, does not imply "a government of laws . . . but a power existing in the people at large, at any time, for any cause, or for no cause, but their own sovereign pleasure, to alter or annihilate both the mode and essence of any government, and adopt a new one in its stead."[25] The Federalists found such ultrademocratic sentiments repugnant, smacking of anarchy and "perpetual vibration," but they did not wholly reject Hichborn's vocabulary.

In fact, the Federalists adopted language like Hichborn's, but with one crucial revision. They agreed, explicitly, that the people could create, alter, or abolish their government when-

23. Lutz, *Popular Consent*, 28–43.
24. Wood, "Conventions of the People," in *Creation*, 344–90.
25. Wood, *Creation*, 362.

ever they chose to do so; but, unlike Hichborn, the Federalists stipulated that, for the acts of "the people" to be valid, they had to act all at once and together. Thus, the Federalists rendered the democratic vocabulary of popular sovereignty harmless by invoking a fictitious people who could not possibly act. The Federalists ascribed all power to a mythical entity that could never meet, never deliberate, never take action. The body politic became a ghost. Once the Federalists had conjured an imaginary "people" who could not challenge the power of the national government, they became bold in declaring that the people had the right to decide, to act, and even to overthrow the government whenever they chose to do so.[26]

Antifederalist theory, in contrast, was based on a localist conception of "the people."[27] In the thought of the Antifederalists, "the people" live in particular places with unique climates and geographies that shape their collective identities; the people take their identities from communities that have their own specific histories, ideals, religions, customs, and manners.[28] Each "people" within the United States, according to the Antifederalists, should have a form of government appropriate to it. The Antifederalists believed that the Federalist conception of "the people" was the basis of a unified nation. Thus, Patrick Henry asked, "Who authorized [the Constitutional Convention] to speak the language of *We, the People*, instead of *We, the States*? States are the characteristics and the soul of a confederation. If the States are not the agents of this compact, it must be one great consolidated national Government of the people of all

26. Ibid., 532.
27. Wilson Carey McWilliams, "Community, Dignity, and the Crisis of Contemporary Politics in America," in *How Democratic Is the Constitution?*, 79–101.
28. Rousseau wrote something remarkably similar to the Antifederalist expressions: "The same laws will not suit so many various provinces, which, with their different customs and contrasting climates, cannot tolerate the same form of government. . . . These general objectives of all institutions must be modified to meet local conditions and suit the character of the people concerned. . . . One must assign to each people the particular form of constitution which is best, not perhaps in itself, but for that state for which it is destined." *The Social Contract*, trans. Maurice Cranston (New York: Penguin Books, 1968), 91, 97.

the States. . . . The people gave them no power to use their name."[29]

In *Federalist* no. 39, Madison tries to refute the Antifederalist charge that the Constitution transforms the American people into a national body politic. He argues there that because the Constitution will be ratified by the states, and because senators will represent the states, the new government is really based on a dual identity of the people, local and national.[30] But Madison's line of reasoning does not convincingly refute Patrick Henry's contention. The direct relationship between the national government and individuals has far more profoundly shaped the political identity of the citizenry than has the method of ratifying the Constitution and the procedures for electing various national officers.[31]

The Federalists describe their concept of a national people in the first several essays of *The Federalist*. They say there that a confederation improperly expresses the identity of "we, the people." To perpetuate the local autonomy guaranteed by the Articles of Confederation would sever the bonds uniting the great American family.

> Providence has been pleased to give this one connected country, to one united people—a people descended from the same ancestors, speaking the same language, professing the same religion, attached to the same principles of government, very similar in their manners and customs. . . . [A] band of brethren, united to each other by the strongest ties, should never be split into a number of

29. *The Complete Anti-Federalist*, 7 vols., ed. Herbert J. Storing (Chicago: University of Chicago Press, 1981), 5.16.1. See also Storing, 3.11.30.

30. *Federalist* no. 39, 254–55.

31. That the Federalists believed the direct relationship to be established between the national government and the citizenry to be crucial to altering the identity of the latter can be deduced from their zealousness in arguing for the establishment of that relationship. See *Federalist* nos. 5, 6, 28, 37:233; Hamilton in Farrand, *Records*, 1:378; Hamilton in *The Papers of Alexander Hamilton*, vol. 1, ed. H. C. Syrett and Jacob E. Cooke (New York: Columbia University Press, 1961), 655–56; Madison in *Mind of the Founder*, ed. Marvin Meyers (Indianapolis: Bobbs-Merrill, 1973), 116.

> unsocial, jealous and alien sovereignties. . . . To all
> general purposes we have uniformly been one people.[32]

John Jay, the third author of *The Federalist,* here indulges in a
bit of mythmaking, deliberately glossing over the variety of
histories, religions, languages, and customs that existed in
America before the Revolution. Jay describes a national identity
that the Constitution was designed to achieve. During the
period of the Articles of Confederation, said historian Merrill
Jensen, a state was a nation in the mind of its citizens.[33] The
Federalists sought to undermine the local loyalty that led citizens to see themselves primarily as members of towns and states
rather than as part of "we the united American people." This
united people, not citizens gathered in towns, counties, and
states, would hereafter wield sovereign power in America; or,
to put it more accurately, the national government would wield
sovereign power in their name.

The Federalists would have denied that they advocated
any sovereignty in the United States except that of the people.
Certainly, no one institution of government would be sovereign, they said, and many subsequent scholars have accepted
their assertions at face value, citing the existence of checks and
balances and the separation of powers. If sovereignty means
absolute, incontrovertible power, as French political theorist
Jean Bodin posited, then it must be conceded that no branch of
the national government is supreme.[34] But an abstract, legalistic
method of reasoning searches for sovereignty in the wrong
way. The Federalists indeed emphasized the division among the
three branches of government when they sought to rebut the
charge that they were creating a highly centralized form of

32. *Federalist* no. 2, 9–10; and no. 14, 88.
33. Merrill Jensen, *The Articles of Confederation* (Madison: University of Wisconsin Press, 1959), 163–64.
34. *Federalist* no. 22, 145; Harold Laski, *Studies in the Problem of Sovereignty* (New
Haven: Yale University Press, 1917), 261–71; Crick, "Sovereignty"; Nannerl O. Keo-
hane, *Philosophy and the State in France* (Princeton: Princeton University Press, 1980),
67–73.

government, but attention to all the writings of Hamilton and Madison reveals the fact that although the Federalists explicitly deny that sovereignty exists in the new government, they also say that is necessary for every government.

In *Federalist* no. 33, Hamilton writes, "But it is said, that the laws of the Union are to be the *supreme law* of the land. But what inference can be drawn from this or what would they amount to, if they were not to be supreme? It is evident they would amount to nothing. . . . [G]overnment . . . is only another word for POLITICAL POWER AND SUPREMACY."[35] Elsewhere he said, "In every society there must be a supreme power, to which all members are subject."[36] Madison, too, wanted to establish "a due supremacy of the national authority, and did not exclude the local authorities wherever they can be subordinately useful."[37] To find the repository of Federalist sovereignty, one should not look to a particular branch of government, nor be misled by Bodin to take absolute supremacy as sovereignty's distinguishing mark. Superior, predominant, but not absolute, power rests in the national government rather than in the states or localities.[38] This superior power is authorized by the Constitution, and the Constitution, in its turn, is sanctioned by its ratification, which was symbolically interpreted as the highest expression of the people's will.[39] The Federalists did not claim that the national government alone derived its power from the people; the states took their power from the same source. They did, however, suggest that the national government's power should be superior to that of the states because it alone spoke for *all* the people, and all the people constituted the genuine body politic of the United

35. *Federalist* no. 33, 207.

36. Hamilton, *Papers* 1:98–99; see also *Federalist* no. 27, 174–75.

37. Madison in Meyers, *Mind*, 95.

38. Garry Wills, *Explaining America* (New York: Penguin Books, 1981), 265–67. Ernest Barker said that Americans chose a "sovereign constitution," in Stourzh, *Hamilton*, 59.

39. See *McCulloch v. Maryland*, 4 Wheat. 316 (1819); Wolin, "The State," 158; *Federalist* no. 78, 524.

States. Each state spoke for only a part of the people, so its will should naturally be subordinated to that of the nation. Because popular sovereignty so greatly reduced the legitimacy of all powers rivaling that of the national government, Tocqueville believed that the doctrine was the greatest catalyst to centralization in the United States. "[Popular] imagination," he said, "conceives of a government which is unitary, protective, and all-powerful, but elected by the people."[40]

The essence of the Federalist doctrine of popular sovereignty is that the supreme power of the national government is sanctioned by the name of the people. In formulating the idea of sovereignty, Hamilton explicitly distinguished between "all members of society" and "a supreme power" to which they are "subject," thus revealing that the Federalists did not intend for the people to actually wield power. Popular sovereignty was a fiction that described a relationship between the people of the United States, conceived of as one body, and the national government. In this relationship the people authorized the government to act in their name and come in direct contact with them, bypassing the states and the localities.[41] The Federalist version of the popular sovereignty doctrine recovered its Hobbesian intention: to describe a single source of power, that is, the individuals who make up society, and the transfer of that power to a central authority. The Federalists said, as did Hobbes, that the power of government flows from the people, but once the people have imparted their power to the national government, then they must refrain from attempting to govern themselves.[42]

In short, the Federalist doctrine of popular sovereignty contained four main elements: (1) the legitimate power of all government comes from the people; (2) "the people" means all

---

40. *Democracy in America*, ed. J. P. Mayer, trans. G. Lawrence (Garden City, N.Y.: Doubleday/Anchor, 1969), 693.

41. *Federalist* no. 14, 93; no. 15, 95.

42. *Federalist* no. 46, 315; Meyers, *Mind*, 151, 153; Walter H. Bennett, *American Theories of Federalism* (University, Alabama: University of Alabama Press, 1964), 85.

citizens of the United States rather than particular groups of citizens joined in political communities and states; (3) because the national government acts in the name of all the people, its legitimacy is superior to that of the states and towns; and (4) because of its direct relationship with all the people, the national government can act upon them without having to go through intermediary bodies. Each of these four propositions serves to increase the power and legitimacy of the national government.

I have suggested that the Federalists invoked the doctrine of popular sovereignty in order to create power for the national government. But why were the Federalists so concerned about a deficiency of power in the new government? And, given their depreciation of democracy, why did they turn to the people to overcome that deficiency? What could popular sanction add to the power created by such institutions as a unitary executive, a national military force, and a national bank? Of what strategy was popular sovereignty a part? To understand the theory of popular sovereignty, one must grasp its politics.

III

The language of popular sovereignty was obviously compelling rhetoric during the ratification debate. Louis Otto, a French diplomat to the United States in the 1780s, wrote home: "It was necessary to agree that all power ought to emanate only from the people; that everything was subject to its supreme will, and that the magistrates were only its servants."[43] Using the vocabulary of popular sovereignty augmented Federalist strength in the combat against their democratic opponents. The logic of the Antifederalist explanation that "we, the people"

43. In Alpheus T. Mason, *The States Rights Debate* (Englewood Cliffs, N.J.: Prentice-Hall, 1964), 28.

created consolidated government "was not very effective in arousing opposition to the plan, for after all, who could object to a government's being made by the people?"[44] Historian Gordon Wood has correctly called the Federalist doctrine of popular sovereignty an effective rhetorical strategy, but he emphasizes the confusing impact Federalist populist language has had on subsequent American thinking rather than recognizing the political significance of the Federalist vocabulary. In Wood's account, the Federalists were guilty of muddling American political thinking because they "expropriated and exploited the language that more rightfully belonged to their opponents. . . . By using the most popular and democratic rhetoric available to explain and justify their aristocratic system, the Federalists helped to foreclose the development of an American intellectual tradition in which differing ideas of politics would be intimately and genuinely related to differing social interests."[45] It is not quite correct to say that the Federalists used "democratic" rhetoric to justify an "aristocracy." Actually, the Federalists employed the traditional language of state-building, which had been temporarily appropriated or misappropriated by democratic localists, to give the projected central government a popular, although not democratic, base. I am not suggesting that the Federalists could have made their antidemocratic intentions more explicit, that they could have openly suggested that the proposed government should be based on something other than the people's will, and still have won ratification of the Constitution. But the Federalist accomplishment in political theory was to turn what might have seemed at the time, and still may seem, to be a concession to popular opinion into a fecund source of power for the national government.

Like the sovereignty of the central government, the Federalist desire to create great national power has been obscured by scholarly concentration on the limits placed by the

44. Jackson Turner Main, *The Antifederalists* (Chapel Hill: University of North Carolina Press, 1961), 122.

45. Wood, *Creation*, 562.

Federalists on the prerogatives of national institutions, particularly the idea of checks and balances.[46] Although the Federalists said that the most important powers of the national government were enumerated rather than implied, they believed that they had enumerated the powers necessary to create a strong central government. And they stated repeatedly that there must be no restraint on the government's enumerated powers.[47] Hamilton said that the powers of raising an army, regulating commerce, and preventing domestic insurrection "ought to exist without limitation. . . . [N]o constitutional shackles can wisely be imposed on the power to which the care of it is committed."[48] And Madison echoed Hamilton's contention: "Where exclusive power is given to the union, there can be no interference."[49] The checks and balances within the national government do not reduce its power. Designed as they were to prevent the immediate enactment of public opinion and to contain the potential damage of corrupt leaders, checks and balances are not incompatible with a strong national government.[50]

Throughout *The Federalist,* Hamilton and Madison exhort the people to overcome their fear of great national power. The very first number of *The Federalist* declares that "the vigour of government is essential to the security of liberty." "Governments destitute of energy, will ever produce anarchy," said Madison. In *The Federalist,* Madison wrote, "Energy in Government is essential." Why were the Federalists so concerned that the new government would lack sufficient power? And why did they fear that the people would not accept a powerful national government?[51] The questions are redundant. If the power of the

46. For discussions of checks and balances, see James MacGregor Burns, *The Deadlock of Democracy* (Englewood Cliffs, N.J.: Prentice-Hall, 1963), and James Sterling Young, *The Washington Community, 1800–1828* (New York: Harcourt, Brace, and World, 1966), esp. 65–86.

47. *Federalist* no. 33, 207.

48. *Federalist* no. 23, 147.

49. Madison, *Papers* 11:122.

50. Wills, *Explaining America,* 162–63.

51. *Federalist* no. 1, 5; Madison, *Papers* 11:93; *Federalist* no. 7, 233. For an alternative understanding of the position held by eighteenth-century Americans concerning power, see Bernard Bailyn, *The Ideological Origins of the American Revolution* (Cambridge: Harvard University Press, Belknap, 1967), 55–93.

national government is seen simply as a means of redressing the inadequacies of the Articles of Confederation, if the Antifederalists are portrayed as "men of little faith," afraid of political power of every kind, then one misses the fact that the Federalists did not merely seek additional power for the national government but sought power of a different kind and a new basis for that power. And one might also fail to take into account what the Federalists took to be the greatest potential peril to the power of the new national government: the scale of the new nation.

The issues of scale and power were connected for the Federalists in complicated ways. The unprecedented scale of a unified America potentially would invest it with an awesome amount of strength, but it also constituted an enormous threat to that strength. The large scale of the United States made extraordinary demands on the central government; to rule over the vast territory of the United States, the central government would have to possess great might. As Hamilton said, only an "energetic government" can "preserve the Union of so large an empire."[52] Where would the energy come from? Whatever additional military and legislative authority might be granted by the Constitution, the ultimate basis for that authority was sought in the creation of a new relationship between the central government and the people, a relationship that I have been calling "popular sovereignty." Popular sovereignty would give the new government the support of the people and, at the same time, insulate the national government from the actual activity of the people. Thus, popular sovereignty would not only constitute a source of national power but establish the condition for its being exercised.

The Federalists believed that a large measure of popular support had to be attained by any government, and they shared the eighteenth-century supposition that popular affection was an essential source of power for a republic. This lesson was

52. *Federalist* no. 23, 151.

driven home by the American Revolution, during which a loose confederation of small states triumphed over the world's greatest empire. The power of republics, said Antifederalist George Mason, came from "the love, the affection, the attachment of the citizens to their laws, to their freedom, and to their country."[53] The Federalists accepted this argument, at least in part, as well as that of Montesquieu, who believed that republics require an active feeling from the people, which he called virtue, whereas monarchies were based on the principle of self-interest.[54] For Hamilton, this was one more good reason for monarchy; he thought, as did the Antifederalists, that only a king could govern a nation as large as the proposed United States. Hamilton said at the Constitutional Convention that he was close to "despair that a Republican Government could be established over so great an extent. He was sensible at the same time that it would be unwise to propose one of any other form. In his private opinion . . . the British Government was the best in the world: and . . . he doubted much whether anything short of it would do in America."[55]

The Federalists feared that even if the people ratified the new government, they might fail to support it because, by nature, most human beings love only small and proximate institutions. So it was highly doubtful that the people would transfer their loyalties from their towns and states to a distant central government.[56] The people, if left to their own devices, would not just neglect the central government, but would support the states instead, thereby providing the latter with power to challenge the supremacy of the national government. Hamilton wrote: "Upon the same principle that a man is more attached to his family than to his neighbourhood, to his neigh-

53. Ferrand, *Records* 1:112.

54. Baron de Montesquieu, *The Spirit of the Laws*, trans. Thomas Nugent (New York: Macmillan, Hafner, 1949), 19–26.

55. Farrand, *Records* 1:288, 299. See also Stourzh, *Hamilton*, 193; "Introduction," in *The Federalist*, ed. B. F. Wright, Jr. (Cambridge: Harvard University Press, 1961), 51.

56. Madison in Meyers, *Mind*, 36; Madison, *Papers*, 1:657–60; *Federalist* no. 45, 311; Farrand, *Records* 1:284–85, 295, 298; Wood, *Creation*, 474, 525.

bourhood than to the community at large, the people of each State would be apt to feel a stronger byass towards their local governments than towards the government of the Union."[57] Madison saw it the same way. The people will care for the localities, he said, because it is

> domestic objects for which people have the strongest predilection. . . . The general government on the contrary has the preservation of the aggregate interests of the union—objects, which being less familiar, and more remote from men's notice, have a less powerful influence on their minds. . . . Do we not see great and natural attachments arising from local considerations? . . . The people will be attached to their state legislatures from a thousand causes; and into whatever scale the people at large will throw themselves, that scale will preponderate.[58]

The Antifederalists analyzed local affection in a similar manner. They agreed that popular affections do not extend very far, that ordinary people support only those governments that reflect their customs. Like the Federalists, the Antifederalists believed that the *natural* repository for those affections was, and would continue to be, the states and communities.[59] But if the Antifederalists and the Federalists each saw parochialism and local political activism as somehow natural, they parted company in deriving political inferences from localism. For the Antifederalists, the geographical limits of patriotism and participation set the natural boundary for the size of a polity. Because people cared only for small governments, and could participate only in small governments, small governments there should be,

57. *Federalist* no. 17, 107; see also Hamilton, *Papers*, 1:655–56; Farrand, *Records* 1:305.

58. Madison, *Papers* 11:115–16.

59. See McWilliams, "Democracy and the Citizen," in *How Democratic Is the Constitution?*

linked loosely in confederation. The alternative, a large consolidated nation, would almost certainly result in tyranny. If the nation replaced the states as the country's essential political form, military coercion would have to substitute for affection to secure the obedience of the populace. If the national government did not fall because of the people's unwillingness to support it, that would mean that the nation's rules had replaced allegiance with force.[60] Antifederalist Richard Henry Lee said that "the general government, far removed from the people . . . , will be forgot or neglected, and its laws in many cases disregarded, unless a multitude of officers and military force be continually kept in view, and employed to enforce the execution of the laws, and to make the government feared and respected."[61]

The Federalists did not dispute the Antifederalist distinction between natural and coerced obedience, nor did they renounce the proposition that natural obedience is given only to small and proximal governments. But the Federalists revealed their theoretical daring and ingenuity by creating a new solution to this traditional political problem.

The Federalists believed that they might have found an alternative to the choice between local patriotism and coercive government. That alternative was popular sovereignty. At the Constitutional Convention, Hamilton said that "only a complete sovereignty in general Government . . . will turn the strong principles and passions" to the central government.[62] He repeated this belief in *The Federalist*: "[E]xtending the authority of the federal head to the individual citizens of the several states . . . will give the Federal Government the same advantage for

60. On the distinction between coercion and legitimate authority, see Hannah Arendt, "What is Authority?" in *Between Past and Future* (New York: Viking, 1968), 91–142, and John H. Schaar, "Legitimacy in the Modern State," in *Legitimacy in the Modern State* (New Brunswick, N.J.: Transaction Press, 1981), 15–52.

61. Storing, *The Complete Anti-Federalist*, 2.8.23.

62. Farrand, *Records*, 1:286. To "transfer the attachment of the people from the governments of their separate states to that of the Union . . . Hamilton advocated an almost complete transfer of sovereignty from the latter governments to the former" (Kenyon, "Rousseau of the Right," 162).

securing a due obedience to its authority, which is enjoyed by the government of each State."[63] Madison also saw sovereignty as a way to secure legitimacy for the national government. He put the point negatively in a critique of the Articles of Confederation. "A sovereignty over sovereigns . . . ," wrote Madison, "is subversive of the order and ends of civil polity, by substituting *violence* in place of *law*, or the destructive *coertion* of the *sword*, in place of the mild and salutary *coertion* of the *magistracy*."[64]

Both Hamilton and Madison believed that national sovereignty might draw the affections of the people to the new government, but they did not clearly specify how this would happen. Popular sovereignty was designed to win public support for the government in three ways: first, rhetorically, by justifying its power in democratic language; second, by establishing the national government as superior to the states and localities; and, finally, by creating a direct relationship between the people and the national government. The Federalists gained widespread affirmation of their new government by being able to claim that it met the populist criterion for legitimacy. Rhetoric reminiscent of democracy evoked assent that produced power. As Tolstoy wrote, "Power is the collective will of the people transferred, by expressed or tacit consent, to their chosen rulers."[65]

The tenet of the popular sovereignty doctrine that generated the most power for the national government was the establishment of a direct relationship between it and the citizenry. Not only did this relationship give the government a stronger means of control over the populace, but the relationship made possible a significant amendment of eighteenth-century political psychology. The traditional political psychology had posited that the people would care only for government

63. *Federalist* no. 27, 174.
64. *Federalist* no. 20, 128–29.
65. Leo Tolstoy, *War and Peace*, trans. Louis and Aylmer Maude, ed. George Gibian (New York: W. W. Norton, 1966), 1323.

near to them. Hamilton modified the definition of "near"; previously, "near," applied to government, had implied institutions located at close geographical proximity to the citizens, but Hamilton thought that the local agents of a national government could achieve the same effect by directly touching the lives of the people. He wrote:

> I will . . . hazard an observation which will not be the less just, because to some it may appear new; which is, that the more the operations of the national authority are intermingled in the ordinary exercise of government; the more the citizens are accustomed to meet with it in the common occurrences of their political life; the more it is familiarised to their sight and to their feelings; the further it enters into those objects which touch the most sensible cords, and put in motion the most active springs of the human heart, the greater will be the probability that it will conciliate the respect and attachment of the community. . . . The more it circulates through those channels and currents, in which the passions of mankind naturally flow, the less will it require the aid of the violent and perilous expedients of compulsion.[66]

If the people could not touch the distant central government, the central government could touch the people. By sending its officers to mingle among the people to tax them and provide them with services, by making themselves familiar, and by becoming the people's primary and most powerful benefactor, the Federalists could win for the national government those popular passions essential to its strength and stability.[67]

66. *Federalist* no. 27, 173–74.
67. In a fascinating chapter of a strong book on the theme of time in early American political thought, *New Order of the Ages: Time, the Constitution, and the Making of Modern American Political Thought* (Princeton: Princeton University Press, 1988), Michael Lienesch describes another path taken by supporters of the Constitution in order to gain its popular acceptance, the reshaping of the American psyche.

IV

The political strategy that produced the Federalist doctrine of popular sovereignty can now be summarized. The Federalists wanted to create a very powerful central government to serve as the cornerstone of a great American empire. Yet, because the new government would be large, distant from the people, and not participatory, the Federalists feared that it would lack one essential source of power: the support of the people. Fear of not attaining this support led both Hamilton and Madison to express discouragement about the potential success of the new government. They pinned their hopes on popular sovereignty. The doctrine of popular sovereignty was both a rhetorical strategy and a new vision of the United States that produced concrete political effects. The ability to claim that the power of the national government came from the people gained power and support for that government in three ways: (1) by undermining the legitimacy of the state governments; (2) by claiming for itself the chief democratic principle of legitimacy—government based on the people; and (3) by directly touching the lives of the people without having to go through the states.

The development of the popular sovereignty doctrine was no small part of the Federalists' political genius. Today this vision has been realized in actual institutions and has gained widespread acceptance, but in the 1780s distant, nonparticipatory, large-scale government was a far more controversial proposition. The Federalists, through the doctrine of popular sovereignty, found a way not only to make their proposed government rhetorically acceptable but to transform that acceptance into a bulwark of the new system. The enormous power of the United States and the nearly universal support for the Constitution are tributes to the potency of Federalist political theory.

At the beginning of this chapter I said that it is necessary to study the Federalists in order to assess contemporary politics accurately. One impediment to judging the condition of democracy in our time is the widely held belief that because the power of the United States government is sanctioned in the name of the people, that power, and the system that produced the power, can therefore be called "democratic." But that assumption is, as we have seen, open to challenge. Admittedly, representative government based on popular sovereignty is more democratic than a monarchy or a government that excludes the people's voice altogether. Nevertheless, the English conception of sovereignty in 1776 is not the proper context for understanding the Federalists' political theory. In 1789 Federalist political thought was not directed against England, but against the localist, participatory, and increasingly egalitarian political order that had developed in the United States. At the heart of the localist political culture were political communities.

The doctrine of popular sovereignty transformed the body politic into a specter. No longer a genuine public, the people could not act. Opponents of democracy were now able to invoke the name of the people without fear of stirring them. Whenever they so desired, Hamilton said, the people could radically alter the government. But "until the people have by some solemn and authoritative act annulled or changed the established form, it is binding upon themselves collectively, as well as individually."[68] Their lack of action, averred Hamilton, commits the citizens to obedience. Until they act, the government is empowered to speak in their name.

But it is impossible for all the citizens of the United States to act together. When a significant minority is organized, national leaders undermine their petitions by appealing to the tacit disagreement of "the silent majority." And if, by prodigious efforts, a majority were to coalesce and in one voice demand significant change, national leaders could then invoke the doctrine of minority rights, or else require the unanimous consent of everyone, the voice of "we, the people" in unison. By attributing sovereignty to a fictitious people, the Federalists

68. *Federalist* no. 78, 527–28; no. 28, 178.

reduced the acts of that people to one: the ratification of the Constitution, symbolically interpreted as an act of the people. After that act the people could only act again when "a general disruption in the federal system or some far-reaching constitutional change was contemplated."[69]

A government that speaks in the name of the people but is not easily changed, is not directly responsive to popular will, and sits at a great distance from the actual lives of most of its citizens may be a good government, even a great government, but it is not a democratic government.

69. Bennett, *American Theories*, 85.

6

Conclusion

In the previous chapters I analyzed a tradition of direct democracy in early America and explored some of the debates concerning democracy at the time of the nation's founding. In each chapter I have tried to suggest the implications of the early debates for thinking about democracy in our own time. I realize that my essay has raised many questions that have thus far gone unanswered: Is democracy, ultimately, a good thing? What is the difference between left-wing democracy and the new federalism advocated by Richard Nixon and Ronald Reagan? What would the recovery of democracy look like? How would forms of politics, work, education, and economy change if they were directly democratic? Would democracy adequately protect the rights of women and minorities? Could a decentralized United States have sufficient military force to protect itself from its enemies? Should the national government

be decentralized without also breaking up the giant corporations? Is democracy in government, the corporation, and the
workplace compatible with a highly competitive and increasingly international economy? In what sense would the United
States be preserved if it decentralized power?

For the time being, these questions must largely remain
unanswered. Each of them is serious and important and de-
serves careful consideration. I simply cannot, in a conclusion,
make the case for direct democracy, fully describe what its
revival might look like, and defend it against its critics. So I
will take the path of indirection: after elaborating some of the
main findings of the previous chapters, I will indicate a few
highlights of the history of direct democracy after 1789 and
suggest a tentative approach to thinking about recovering democracy today.

I

In early America democracy was more than a theoretical matter, it was a way of life; so discussions about democracy and
localism always had an institutional dimension. When they
arrived in America, the Puritans had to determine how to put
into practice the localist ideas they had developed in England
concerning church organization and membership. In the next
century democracy permeated every aspect of the political
culture, taking the form not only of direct action but also of
state constitutions that broadly distributed power and a political
economy that preserved autonomous face-to-face communities.
Those communities were the fundamental institutional component of the Antifederalist political ideal. The Antifederalists
thought that each type of community should have a form of
government appropriate to it, rather than being subject to
transformation by a distant central government.

The Federalists had a much different vision of the United States than did the localists. The Federalists rejected direct democracy as an inappropriate type of government for a powerful nation. They said that democracy brought out the worst in people, inciting them to zealotry and anarchy. As a substitute for democracy, they proposed a set of institutions that embodied the more undemocratic aspects of liberalism, valuing the insulation of rulers from the people and checks and balances in government instead of broadly distributed power, equality of condition, and community. Their proposals were couched in terms similar to those of radical democracy.

What can be learned about democracy's nature and promise in our own time from studying its incarnation in early America? Perhaps the most basic lesson is the one taught by all early localists: democracy is a political structure that entrusts ordinary people with power. Therefore, the first concern in a democracy is always the character and activity of the citizens. Rousseau wrote, "People forget that houses may make a town, while only citizens make a city."[1] Rousseau's statement articulates the theme of collective identity that preoccupied early American democrats.

Today cities and nations are not defined by individual members, but by their institutions and representative figures. When the President of the United States acts, he does so in the name of the whole country. Similarly, the mayor and city council members stand for the body politic in the execution of their duties, as do police officers, who wear badges on their uniforms saying, "City of —." In modern liberal regimes the president, mayor, and police officer participate in the identity of the nation or city in a more fundamental way than do ordinary citizens. One reason that city and national officials must run for election, and that police officers must take a test to attain their positions and then undergo training, is that they in a certain sense embody the city.

1. *The Social Contract,* ed. Maurice Cranston (New York: Penguin Books, 1968), 61.

Conversely, because individual citizens do not constitute the city's identity, they are free to come and go, to move in and out of the city as they please.[2] Most people take the right of mobility for granted and do not consciously realize the political price they have paid for their freedom. When individual members are no longer essential to the identity of the body politic and that identity is transferred to institutions and representatives, leaders gain practically unlimited power because they can claim abstract authority for their actions.

The democratic task, then, is to make the power of ordinary people direct and literal rather than abstract and symbolic. This assertion leads inevitably to the core issue: Are ordinary citizens now, and were they ever, competent to rule themselves directly? Unfortunately, most modern thought about democracy is divided between those who say that citizens are capable of choosing their own representatives and those who say that they are not. The argument that citizens cannot govern themselves leads to the question: What constitutes the qualifications of citizens to wield power at all, even that of choosing and judging their representatives?

To address this issue one must ask: What does the ordinary citizen, who has perhaps not attended college, know? What in the individual's experience has equipped him or her to debate public matters wisely, to hold a sensible opinion, or to vote intelligently? One approach to answering these questions distinguishes between experiential and abstract knowledge. Although not everyone has undertaken a formal program of study, everyone by the age of eighteen or so has accumulated experience and a body of knowledge based on this experience. A great deal of knowledge, if not wisdom, is acquired through such typical experiences as growing up, developing and preserv-

---

2. This freedom of mobility is not only an element in American political thinking as described by, say, D. H. Lawrence in "The Spirit of Place," *Studies in Classic American Literature* (New York: Penguin, 1977 [1923]), 7–14. It has also been written into law. See *Edwards v. California*, 314 U.S. 160, and *Shapiro v. Thompson*, 394 U.S. 618.

ing relationships with others, getting through school, facing temptation, finding work and career, taking on a complex variety of conflicting social roles, confronting illness, loss, and death. For many people, some form of public activity, perhaps not explicitly called political, is part of their ordinary experience. They work with others, engage in debate, negotiate, and take action as part of groups in their schools, clubs, churches, unions, and communities. Today, however, knowledge acquired from experience is taken to be little or no part of the mental equipment required for political rule. To understand and competently address complex matters of government is thought to require technical training in law, international relations, and economics.

This differentiation of two types of knowledge, experiential and technical, has been a central concern of phenomenology, and so it is appropriate to turn for further clarification to a neglected essay on mass political thinking by the phenomenologist Alfred Schutz. Schutz thought that citizens could rule themselves, but not all citizens without qualification could do so. Schutz thought that power should rest with the "well-informed citizen" who has reasonably founded opinions on subjects of concern to him or her rather than with "the man on the street" who has done little or no thinking about public matters.[3] Schutz wrote, "It is the well-informed citizen who considers himself perfectly qualified to decide who *is* a competent expert and to make up his mind after having listened to opposing expert opinions." Schutz believed that the opinion of the "man on the street," which is public opinion as it is understood nowadays, has gained ever more social approval at the expense of informed opinion. A certain tendency to misinterpret democracy as a political institution in which the opinion of the uninformed "man on the street" must predominate increases the danger of poor political judgments. It is the duty

3. Alfred Schutz, "The Well-Informed Citizen: An Essay on the Social Distribution of Knowledge," in Arvid Broderson, ed., *Studies in Social Theory,* vol. 2 of *The Collected Papers of Alfred Schutz* (The Hague: Martinus Nijhoff, 1964), 120–34.

and the privilege, therefore, of the well-informed citizen in a democratic society, says Schutz, to make his or her opinion prevail over the opinion of the "man on the street."[4]

Must a theory of democracy that is based on a respect for experiential or tacit knowledge attempt to refute Schutz and argue that the opinion of uninformed and uninvolved people on public matters should be the basis of government? One democratic answer is, yes, people have enough knowledge from typical experience to govern. But an important tradition within democratic theory, a tradition that includes the Antifederalists, Tocqueville, Josiah Royce, Mary Parker Follett, and Hannah Arendt, does not make such an argument. These theorists believed that political participation with others, not just voting or expressing an opinion, constitutes a form of experience that works a change upon the consciousnesses of citizens, elevating them from a private to a public field of vision.[5] Paradoxically, democratic theorists have suggested that the best school for citizens is participation itself. When people escape the confinement of their solitary lives and act with others in public life, their vision will be broadened. In a direct democracy, experience itself transforms the "man on the street" into a well-informed citizen. Political activity is the civic education that qualifies citizens to rule themselves. Democracy provides the education for democracy.

Moreover, one should not place so much emphasis on the need for preparation to rule that one makes the mistake of saying that the people are unqualified to govern without being reformed. To be a democrat means to see the people for what they can be and, at the same time, to accept people for what

4. Ibid., 123, 134.

5. Mary Parker Follett, *The New State: Group Organization the Solution of Popular Government* (Gloucester, Mass.: Peter Smith, 1965 [1918]); Alexis de Tocqueville, *Democracy in America,* ed. J. P. Mayer, trans. G. Lawrence (Garden City, N.Y.: Doubleday/Anchor, 1969), 61–70, 509–13; Josiah Royce, *The Philosophy of Loyalty* (New York: Hafner, 1971 [1908]); and Hannah Arendt, *The Human Condition* (Chicago: University of Chicago Press, 1958), esp. 7–78. See also Joshua Miller, "No Success Like Failure: Existential Politics in Norman Mailer's *The Armies of the Night,*" *Polity* 22 (Spring 1990): 379–96.

they are. The Antifederalists taught the importance of respecting local, even parochial knowledge. It is an article of democratic faith that adults should have the power to make the decisions that affect their lives.[6]

A second lesson to be learned from early American politics is that democracy pertains not only to formally political institutions, such as parties and elections, but to all aspects of political culture. A genuine democracy requires egalitarian arrangements for work, education, business, agriculture, and the military. Too often in our society, formal guarantees of equality in the public sphere are undermined by hierarchy and discrimination in private life.[7]

The Federalists themselves have important lessons to teach citizens today. By carefully reading the Federalist writings and speeches we can better attain collective self-knowledge. The Federalist revolution was more than just a consolidation of the states, more than the creation and affirmation of the Constitution. Rather, the Federalists induced a permanent, comforting confusion into American political thinking. The Federalists misled the citizenry into believing that large, distant government was compatible with genuinely popular rule. Thus, the hallmark of democracy came to be elections and the protection of individual rights, instead of the actual rule of the people through participation in governing. The large scale of the new nation created in 1789, along with the antidemocratic provisions of the Constitution, soon rendered popular sovereignty a fiction, a myth that legitimated the power of the national government. As Madison correctly asserted in *Federalist* no. 10, a people spread out over a vast area could not unite to challenge the power of the national government. The rhetoric of popular

6. I was once at a conference on early American politics where a government official patiently explained to me the problem with direct democracy: "It's like allowing children in a candy store to eat everything they see." I suggested that his analogy was inappropriate for adults.

7. "On the Jewish Question," in *Karl Marx: Early Writings,* ed. T. Bottomore (New York: McGraw-Hill, 1964), 1–40; Samuel Bowles and Herbert Gintis, *Schooling in Capitalist America* (New York: Basic Books, 1976).

sovereignty was employed by national leaders to undermine the reality of direct democracy, which up to that time had been embodied in political institutions and participatory practices. Discourse about democracy has been muddled ever since.

Studying the debates about early American politics should clarify democracy's nature. In principle, the key elements of democracy are participation, power, community, and equality. Democracy requires autonomy, stability, and a government whose operations ordinary people can understand. In practice, these elements are, admittedly, not always found together. Some autonomous communities, for example, are not egalitarian or participatory. But this is only to say that democracy is an ideal, a goal toward which we may strive, not a program that can be perfectly achieved.[8]

II

Democracy in America is not what it used to be. When Tocqueville visited the United States in 1830, he was impressed by the amount and extent of political activity in local communities. He wrote "[I]f an American should be reduced to occupying himself with his own affairs, at that moment half his existence would be snatched from him; he would feel it as a vast void in his life and would become incredibly unhappy."[9] At some point between 1830 and the present, the American political character changed. Tocqueville's statement no longer accurately characterizes the relationship of the average American to civic life. On the contrary, most Americans would feel that their existence would be greatly diminished if they were forced to become

8. See Charles Douglas Lummis, "The Radicalism of Democracy," *democracy* 2 (1982): 9–16.
9. *Democracy in America*, 243.

involved in public life, or to stay informed about politics, or—
as in some countries citizens are required to do by law—simply
to vote.[10]

In the absence of a vigorous public life, many people
have grown resigned to their lack of power, while others move
from outrage to despair to apathy as responses to the sense that
they cannot affect the decisions made in their name by the
government. Many citizens experienced feelings of helpless-
ness, and perhaps even shame, in response to the conduct of the
war in Vietnam, the bombing of Cambodia, the invasions of
Grenada and Panama, and the actions of the national government in Nicaragua and El Salvador. That same feeling of
powerlessness is felt by citizens whose neighborhoods are rav-
aged by drugs and crime, and by those who want to prevent
the plundering of the environment and the destruction of many
species of life on the planet.

Some will say that if citizens had sufficient will and
virtue they could unite, even under the present regime, to take
action on these issues, as they have done in many instances.
Lack of public virtue, not faulty governmental design, is the
problem. I partly agree, but I tend not to place the blame for
withdrawal from politics on the people themselves. Popular
resignation should be seen as the result, largely, of Federalist
political thought, national and local institutions calculated to
frustrate popular action, and the large scale of the nation.[11]
People tend to withdraw from politics not because they naturally prefer private life to public, but because the political
amateur seems powerless to make an impact. Attempting to do
so on the local, state, or national level, through mainstream or

10. See Michael Oreskes, "Today's Youth Cares Less for Worries of the World,"
New York Times, 28 June 1990, A1.
11. I do not mean that the Federalists sought the low level of public virtue that
we have today. They tried to persuade their fellow citizens to refrain from fervent
political activity, but could not have imagined that they would be as successful as they
were. Madison later regretted the effects of large-scale government on public character.
Hamilton's fantasies in *The Federalist* of conflict between the people and the national
government are all based on a highly aware and energetic populace.

alternative political means, requires forsaking everything else. Generally, one needs to be a person of considerable means to make a political career, either to live on the low wages that are generally paid to those who work full-time for political causes or to undertake a serious campaign for state or national public office. And then, should an individual make the sacrifice of time and money, what effect is one likely to have, given the size of the nation and the hideously complex system of checks, balances, and divisions of power? I do not want to imply that politics is an unworthy activity; on the contrary, to advocate democracy is to recommend politics to nearly everyone. But under present conditions, politics requires a full-time commitment that precludes the amateurism that is at the heart of democracy.

It should be clear by now that the United States is not a direct democracy and has never claimed to be one. In the eighteenth century there was a fierce debate over the question whether or not the United States should continue to be a direct democracy, and the democrats lost. This does not mean, however, that the story of American democracy ended with the ratification of the Constitution. The transformation from the highly participatory and communitarian political culture of early America to the culture of today did not occur in 1789. The Federalist Constitution created a theoretical and institutional framework for a victory over direct democracy that would not be fully realized until after the Civil War. Describing how technology, economics, the federal courts, and the rise of the welfare/warfare state contributed to centralization's triumph is beyond the scope of this essay, as is a detailed account of various theoretical and political attempts to recover direct democracy since 1789.[12] Nevertheless, the democratic tradition,

12. On the rise of the state, see *The Education of Henry Adams,* ed. E. Samuel (Boston: Houghton Mifflin, Riverside Editions, 1973 [1918]); Eric Foner, *Reconstruction, 1863–1877: America's Unfinished Revolution* (New York: Harper and Row, Perennial Library, 1988); and Gabriel Kolko, *The Triumph of Conservatism* (New York: Free Press, 1963).

or at least its high points, can be outlined here. I will say a bit more about recent movements than the earlier ones.

Any study of genuine democracy after the Constitution would have to attend to the following:

1. The New England tradition of town meetings, which has lasted into the twentieth century.[13]

2. Jefferson's proposals for dividing the nation into ward republics.[14]

3. The Whiskey and the Dorr rebellions.[15]

4. State and local challenges to national power, including the Nullification Crisis and the Virginia and Kentucky resolutions.[16]

5. The states' rights arguments made by nineteenth-century abolitionists in order to prevent the extension of slavery into the territories and the national government from forcing obedience to the Fugitive Slave Law.[17]

6. Nineteenth-century political parties.[18]

7. The Knights of Labor.[19]

13. Page Smith, *As a City Upon a Hill* (New York: Knopf, 1966); Richard R. Lingeman, *Small Town America: A Narrative History* (New York: Putnam, 1980).

14. Thomas Jefferson to Samuel Kercheval, 12 July 1816, in *The Portable Thomas Jefferson*, ed. Merrill D. Peterson (New York: Viking, 1975). See also Richard K. Matthews, *The Radical Politics of Thomas Jefferson* (Lawrence: University Press of Kansas, 1984), 77–89, and Garrett Sheldon, *The Political Philosophy of Thomas Jefferson* (Baltimore: Johns Hopkins University Press, 1991).

15. Thomas P. Slaughter, *The Whiskey Rebellion* (New York: Oxford University Press, 1986); Marvin E. Gettleman, *The Dorr Rebellion: A Study in American Radicalism, 1833–1849* (New York: Random House, 1973).

16. Thomas Jefferson, "The Kentucky Resolutions," in *The Portable Jefferson*, 281–89; James Madison, "Republican Manifesto: the Virginia Report," in *Mind of the Founder: Sources of the Political Thought of James Madison*, ed. Marvin Meyers (Indianapolis: Bobbs-Merrill, 1973), 297–349.

17. Eric Foner, *Free Soil, Free Labor, Free Men* (New York: Oxford, 1970), 134–39 and passim.

18. William Riordon, *Plunkitt of Tammany Hall* (New York: E. P. Dutton, 1963 [1905]); Walter Dean Burnham, *Critical Elections and the Mainsprings of American Politics* (New York: Norton, 1970); Michael E. McGeer, *The Decline of Popular Politics* (New York: Oxford University Press, 1986).

19. Leon Fink, *Workingmen's Democracy: The Knights of Labor and American Politics* (Urbana and Chicago: University of Illinois Press, 1983).

8. The Populists or People's Party.[20]

9. Theorists of the Progressive era, including Randolph Bourne, John Dewey, Lewis Mumford, and Mary Parker Follett.[21]

10. While much African-American political thought, most prominently that of Frederick Douglass and Martin Luther King, Jr., has criticized the national government for not requiring integration, ending slavery and discrimination, and offering compensation for past wrongs, there has also been a strain in black political thought that emphasizes community self-determination.[22] Alain Locke's *When Peoples Meet* is a central text on ethnic diversity. Malcolm X, Stokely Carmichael, the Student Nonviolent Coordinating Committee, and advocates of community control, like Mel King in Boston and activists in the painful Ocean-Hill Brownsville case have put self-determination rather than integration or national intervention at the top of their political agenda.[23]

20. Lawrence Goodwyn, *The Populist Moment: A Short History of the Agrarian Revolt in America* (New York: Oxford University Press, 1978); C. Vann Woodward, *Tom Watson: Agrarian Rebel* (New York: Macmillan, 1938), and *Origins of the New South* (Baton Rouge: Louisiana State University Press, 1971 [1951]).

21. Bourne developed a theory of democratic diversity in his essay "Trans-National America," in *War and the Intellectuals: Essays by Randolph S. Bourne,* ed. Carl Resek (New York: Harper and Row, 1964), 107–23. Mary Parker Follett envisioned a new America based on active political communities in her great book, *The New State.* See also John Dewey, *The Public and Its Problems* (Chicago: Swallow Press, 1954); Lewis Mumford, "A Search for the True Community," in Leo Schwartz, ed., *The Menorah Treasury* (Philadelphia: Jewish Publication Society, 1964), 857–67; Philip Selznick, *TVA and the Grass Roots* (Berkeley: University of California Press, 1949); and Casey Nelson Blake, *Beloved Community: The Culture Criticism of Randolph Bourne, Van Wyck Brooks, Waldo Frank, and Lewis Mumford* (Chapel Hill: University of North Carolina Press, 1990).

22. See V. P. Franklin, *Black Self-Determination* (Westport, Conn.: Lawrence Hill, 1984).

23. On SNCC, see Clayborne Carson, *In Struggle: SNCC and the Black Awakening of the Nineteen Sixties* (Cambridge: Harvard University Press). See also Alain Locke, *When Peoples Meet* (New York: Committee on Workshops, Progressive Education Association, 1942); *Malcolm X. Speaks,* ed. George Breitman (New York: Grove-Weidenfeld, 1976); Stokely Carmichael and Charles Hamilton, *Black Power* (New York: Vintage, 1967); J. Anthony Lukas, *Common Ground* (New York: Knopf, 1985); Philip Green, "Decentralization, Community Control and Revolution: Reflections on Ocean-Hill Brownsville," in *Power and Community: Dissenting Essays in Political Science,* ed. Philip Green and Sanford Levinson (New York: Vintage, 1970), 247–75; and Mel King, *Chain of Change: Struggles for Black Community Development* (Boston: South End Press, 1981).

11. The 1960s witnessed a major resurgence of the ideal of direct democracy. The founding document of the Students for a Democratic Society, the Port Huron Statement, called for "participatory democracy."[24] "Student power" became a lively cause in many high schools and colleges, as students sought to take part in shaping the curriculum, in the hiring and firing of teachers, and in institutional governance.[25]

12. The community organizing movement tries to attain power for the poor and lower middle class by developing neighborhood groups that take direct action and lobby local, state, and national government officials.[26]

13. Feminism is part of the direct democracy movement. Feminists have been highly critical of arbitrary forms of hierarchy, and they generally distrust inequality. Feminists also stress the values of community and democratic process in political decision making. Some feminists see competitive individualism as a masculine characteristic and associate women with more cooperative relationships. They criticize modern society for being "hyper-masculine," and would recover community by going in "womanist" directions.[27] Feminists have also called attention to the nature of the political process, that is, the means by which political groups achieve their ends.

24. The Port Huron Statement is reprinted in James Miller, *Democracy Is in the Streets: From Port Huron to the Siege of Chicago* (New York: Simon and Schuster, 1987). See also Kirkpatrick Sale, *SDS* (New York: Random House, 1973); Todd Gitlin, *The Sixties* (New York: Bantam, 1987); and Tom Hayden, *Reunion: A Memoir* (New York: Random House, 1988).

25. *The New Student Left*, ed. Mitchell Cohen and Dennis Hale (Boston: Beacon Press, 1967).

26. Saul Alinsky's *Reveille for Radicals* (New York: Random House, 1969 [1946]) is a central text for that movement. See Harry C. Boyte, *Backyard Revolution* (Philadelphia: Temple University Press, 1980); Frances Fox Piven and Richard A. Cloward, *Poor People's Movements* (New York: Vintage, 1979); and Gary Delgado's *Organizing the Movement: The Roots and Growth of ACORN* (Philadelphia: Temple University Press, 1986). SDS's role in the community-organizing movement is described in James Miller, *Democracy*, 201–17, and Wini Breines, *Community and Organization in the New Left, 1962–1968* (New York: Praeger, Bergin & Garvey, 1982).

27. See Starhawk, *Dreaming the Dark: Magic, Sex, and Politics* (Boston: Beacon Press, 1982), esp. 92–102; Carol Gilligan, *In a Different Voice* (Cambridge: Harvard University Press, 1982); and Wendy Brown, *Manhood and Politics* (Totowa, N.J.: Rowman & Littlefield, 1988).

Feminists have argued that communitarian and democratic ends cannot be attained through hierarchical, agonistic organizations. This attention to process and the critique of hierarchy are, to my mind, two of the most important areas for democratic study today.[28]

14. Experiments in worker ownership and worker participation in plant decision making have potential for contributing to an egalitarian political culture.[29]

15. The consumer movement personified by Ralph Nader has encouraged the overcoming of deference in the marketplace.[30]

16. Radical union movements including Teamsters for a Democratic Union, dissidents in the United Auto Workers, and Hospital Workers Local 1199.[31]

17. Movements by gays and the physically disabled have extended the boundaries of equal citizenship.[32]

18. The environmental movement is truly conservative in its effort to preserve nature and the various species of plant and wildlife on the planet. In doing so, environmentalists have

28. See Sara Evans, *Personal Politics* (New York: Vintage, 1980), and Barbara Epstein, "The Culture of Direct Action: Livermore Action Group and the Peace Movement," *Socialist Review* 81 (May/June 1985): 31–61. See also essays by Charlene Spretnak, "Postmodern Populism: The Greening of Technocratic Society," 156–64; Elizabeth Kamarack Minnich, "Toward a Feminist Populism," 191–97; Kathy E. Ferguson, *The Feminist Case Against Bureaucracy* (Philadelphia: Temple University Press, 1984); and Mary G. Dietz, "Populism, Patriotism and the Need for Roots," in *The New Populism: The Politics of Empowerment*, ed. Harry C. Boyte and Frank Riessman (Philadelphia: Temple University Press, 1986), 261–73.

29. Christopher Gunn, *Workers' Self-Management in the United States* (Ithaca: Cornell University Press, 1984); Catherine J. Ivancic and John Logue, "Democratizing the American Corporation: Illusion and Realities of Employee Participation and Ownership" (unpublished paper).

30. Frank Riessman, "The New Populism and the Empowerment Ethos," in *The New Populism*, 53–63.

31. See Kim Moody, *An Injury to All: The Decline of American Unionism* (London: Verso, 1988); Hardy Green, *On Strike at Hormel: The Struggle for a Democratic Labor Movement* (Philadelphia: Temple University Press, 1989); and Leon Fink and Brian Greenberg, *Upheaval in the Quiet Zone: A History of Hospital Workers Union, Local 1199* (Urbana and Chicago: University of Illinois Press, 1989).

32. Randy Shilts, *And the Band Played On: Politics, People, and the AIDS Epidemic* (New York: St. Martin's Press, 1987); Adrienne Asch, "Will Populism Empower Disabled People?" in *The New Populism*, 191–97.

challenged economic and technological imperatives for incessant development and change.[33]

19. The tenant management movement in public housing.[34]

20. As wrongheaded as they may seem, many apparently reactionary groups have a democratic dimension in that they resist the dissemination of values and culture from sources in Los Angeles, New York, and Washington. The goals of these movements for cultural autonomy include: school prayer, control over curriculum including classes taught in their own languages, creationism, and opposition to sex education and pornography.[35]

These different types of political activity may not all be democratic in every sense of the word, or valid on other grounds, but they each preserve one or more elements of early American democracy. The list shows that after the mid-nineteenth century, direct democracy may no longer have been a constituent element of mainstream politics, but was central to many of the most significant political efforts in the nation's history. Direct democracy has been diminished, but not vanquished.

III

Impatient with theory and historical description, the sympathetic reader insistently asserts, "I agree with what you say . . .

33. Christopher Manes, *Green Rage: Radical Environmentalism and the Unmaking of Civilization* (Boston: Little, Brown, 1990); Wendell Berry, *The Unsettling of America: Culture and Agriculture* (San Francisco: Sierra Club Books, 1977); William Greider, "California's Big Green Brings the Law to Earth," *Rolling Stone*, 23 August 1990, 53–56.

34. Harry C. Boyte, "People Power Transforms a St. Louis Housing Project," *Utne Reader*, July/August 1989, 46–47; Bill Peterman, "New Options for Resident Control," *Shelterforce* 10 (January/February 1987): 14–15; William A. Peterman, "Resident Management," *Journal of Housing* 45 (May/June, 1988): 111–15; Robert L. Koenig, "Carr Square at the Center of Housing Debate," *St. Louis Post-Dispatch*, 2 November 1989; Robert Koenig, "Law Change Sought for Tenant Group," *St. Louis Post-Dispatch*, 8 March 1989.

35. See Sheldon S. Wolin, "Archaism, Modernity, and *Democracy in America*," in *The Presence of the Past: Essays on the State and the Constitution* (Baltimore: Johns Hopkins University Press, 1989), 79–80.

but I wish you would consider what we ought to *do*."[36] I can offer only these compressed formulations: People who want to create or experiment with democracy should begin where they are. They should try to give more power to, and seek more participation from, all members of a workplace, community, or organization. Everyone's skills and education should be attended to; no one should be looked upon as simply a means to help others do the important work.

As I have suggested, the following groups might be among the agents of democratic change: students, workers, citizen-activists, feminists, racial minorities, members of religious groups, the physically disabled, and environmentalists. Members of these groups may not know each other, and in fact may harbor deep prejudices against each other, but they share a cause that transcends their particular issues. In order for them to recognize their common cause, people will have to bridge deep divisions of worldview in our culture, divisions among races and religions, between the sexes, between those living in urban and rural areas, those who live on the coasts and those who reside in the South and Midwest. Those who want to train for democracy should learn as much as they can about their own traditions and also about the cultures of those unlike themselves in the United States and abroad. Democracy implies embracing one's own identity and respecting those who are different.[37]

What should be done at the national level? Gar Alperovitz suggests that the national government should be reduced to a set of regional administrations.[38] Plans of partial disunion are needed that give more autonomy to regions, states, cities,

36. Plato, "The Crito," *The Last Days of Socrates,* trans. Hugh Tredennick (New York: Penguin Books, 1954), 87.

37. Randolph Bourne and Abraham Lincoln are the best teachers here. See John H. Schaar, "The Case for Patriotism," in *Legitimacy in the Modern State* (New Brunswick, N.J.: Transaction Press, 1981), 285–311.

38. "Toward a Tough-Minded Populism," in *The New Populism,* 169.

boroughs, and neighborhoods.[39] Obviously, the national government cannot be safely ignored, but too much energy should not be spent trying to make change at that level. It is too difficult, by design, to make national change, and attempting to do so will deplete political energy. And there is a danger that national reform will replicate the same hierarchical, centralist, disciplinary politics that localists seek to overturn. Images of total revolution, especially from the top down, should be rejected. No central committee can devise and carry out the campaign for direct democracy.

Is there any possibility that our country can move in a decentralist direction? This is not the first question. The real debate, it seems to me, is over whether change is preferable, not whether it is possible. We could live differently if we had the will. Ironically, democrats could take the Federalists as a model. Like decentralists today, the Federalists had a vastly different vision of what the United States should look like than did most of their contemporaries. Others thought that a centralized republican government over an expansive territory was impossible, but the Federalists developed a theoretical argument for change, wrote a constitution that gave institutional embodiment to those innovations, and employed a sophisticated political strategy to gain popular assent for their plans. Decentralists today must reject despair and imitate the Federalists' vision and resolution.

To do so will require courage and patience. Like all radicals, conservative democrats will face fierce opposition when they begin to act. Direct democracy is a highly threatening doctrine. The costs of advocating it in one's corporation, workplace, union, neighborhood, city, or school could be great. With a due regard for Machiavelli's counsel to friends of

39. Robert Goodman, *The Last Entrepreneurs* (Boston: South End Press, 1982); Kirkpatrick Sale, *Dwellers in the Land: The Bioregional Vision* (San Francisco: Sierra Club Books, 1985); Milton Kotler, *Neighborhood Government* (Indianapolis: Bobbs-Merrill, 1969).

liberty that those who would make political change would do well to survive first, I still believe that we should try.

We must be at once eager for political transformation and patient because sometimes change seems impossible. Luckily, this is a time of great social and political transformations, although, oddly enough, not in the United States. It once seemed sure that he would die there, but Nelson Mandela has been released from jail, and apartheid in South Africa appears to be crumbling. Many former democratic dissidents in Eastern Europe left jail to take positions of power in their governments. The Berlin Wall has been torn down. The Soviet Union for the first time in its history is having free elections and permitting a measure of free speech. If nothing else, these examples show that institutions are not as permanent and impregnable as they sometimes seem, that great political action is still possible. We could take the path of democracy if we chose it.

Index